From Wales to Pe
~ The David Thomas

by Peter N. Williams, Ph.D

Wales Books
Glyndŵr Publishing
2002

Copyright 2002 Dr Peter N. Williams

Published in 2002 by Wales Books (Glyndŵr Publishing),
Porth Glyndŵr, Sain Tathan, Bro Morgannwg CF62 4LW
www.walesbooks.com

The right of Peter N. Williams to be identified as the Author of this Work has been asserted by him in accordance with the Copyright, Designs and Patents Act 1988.

All rights reserved. No part of this publication may be reproduced, stored in a retrieval system or transmitted, in any form or by any means, without the prior permission of the publisher, nor be otherwise circulated in any form of binding or cover other than that in which it is published and without similar condition being imposed on the subsequent purchaser.

A CIP catalogue record for this book is available from the British Library.

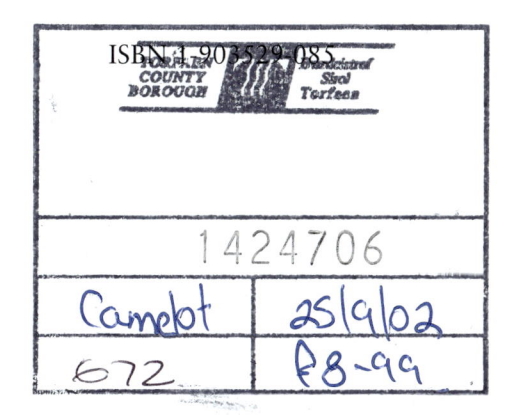

ISBN 1-903529-085

Printed and bound in Wales by
J & P Davison, 3 James Place,
Trefforest, Pontypridd CF37 1SQ

About the Author

Peter N. Williams was born in Mancot, a little village in Flintshire, North Wales, just inside the border with England. Brought up in the industrial town of Flint, he was educated at King's School, Chester and at the University College, Swansea, South Wales.

After arriving in the United States in 1957, he served with the US Army in Germany with an artillery unit. Following his military service, he taught high school in Delaware for a number of years before completing his Ph.D. in English at the University of Delaware. He then taught English at the university before becoming chairman of the English department at Delaware Technical and Community College. He is now the editor of Celticinfo.com.

Founder of the Welsh Society of Delaware, Peter was honored for his work on behalf of Wales and Welsh Americas by being made a member of the Gorsedd at the national Eisteddfof of Wales in 1999. Peter is the author of *The Sacred Places of Wales* and the editor of *38 Hymns in Welsh and English*.

From Wales to Pennsylvania
~ The David Thomas Story ~

Table of Contents

		Page
Chapter One:	May, 1839: Ystradgynlais to Liverpool	1
Chapter Two:	Developments at Ynyscedwyn	5
Chapter Three:	Rails and Ships of Iron	14
Chapter Four:	The Early Iron Industry in Pennsylvania	18
Chapter Five:	The Atlantic Crossing	25
Chapter Six:	The Age of the Iron Steamship	30
Chapter Seven:	Conditions in Wales: Unemployment, Drink, and Temperance	39
Chapter Eight:	The Chartist Movement	48
Chapter Nine:	The Newport Rising	54
Chapter Ten:	More Troubled Times in Wales	65
Chapter Eleven:	The Question of the Welsh Language	73
Chapter Twelve:	David Thomas: Industrial Giant	81
Chapter Thirteen:	Man of Might: Papa Thomas	91

Foreword

This book was originally titled *David Thomas: Iron Man from Wales. The Story of an Immigrant and of the Country he left Behind*, published by NWAF, l995. This book was written chiefly from a collection of 29 letters to David Thomas at Allentown, Pennsylvania from his former employer, George Crane; his family, his friends and workmates in Ystradgynlais, South Wales. The original letters, which cover the period May 6, 1839 to February 28, 1842, are kept at the Hagley Museum, Wilmington, Delaware.

For this edition, retitled from the orignial, I have added addtional photographs, additional material, and have made corrections and revisons. Use of a larger font has also made the text more readable

A great deal of information about events in Wales during that period was derived from the mid-nineteenth century Welsh newspaper, *The Cambrian*, published at Swansea, South Wales.

In addition to those who provided help in the original edition, I am indebted to Mr. Mansel Jones, of Ystradgynlais, for providing important details about David's early life and a copy of the contract between David and the Lehigh Navigation and Coal Company.

In turn, on behalf of Mr. Jones, I wish to thank Mr. David Ley, also of Ystradgynlais for providing some necessary information. I also wish to thank Mrs. Ruth Thomas May, great, great grand daughter of David for photographs of the sailing ship Roscius, the Thomas home in Catasauqua, Pennsylvania, and a portrait of David.

Chapter One

Farewell to the Swansea Valley

It was May, 1839. David Thomas, his wife Jane, with their three boys and two girls, had just arrived at the Liverpool Landing Stage to board their ship that would take them all to a new life in America. "Wel, nghariad a fy mhlant i, dyna chi. Edrychwch ar ein llong brydferth newydd" (Well, my love, and my children, look at our beautiful new ship).

Speaking excitedly in Welsh to his wife and children, David pointed excitedly in the direction of the sailing ship *Roscius*, on which they would travel across the Atlantic Ocean. Sleek, gleaming and proud, her finely sculptured lines made her stand out conspicuously among the scores of ships anchored alongside in the Waterloo Dock, Liverpool, from where the fast new American clipper ships were taking thousands of emigrants to the United States.

The family had arrived in Liverpool from Swansea on the *Mountaineer* on the first leg of the journey that would eventually take them across the Atlantic to begin a new life in Pennsylvania. There, David was to begin work in Allentown as an iron master with the newly-formed Lehigh Crane Iron Company which had invited him over on a five-year contract.

For more than twenty years, David had been employed at the Ynyscedwyn Iron Works at the little town of Ystradgynlais in the Swansea Valley. Saying goodbye to all their friends, and giving a special hug to Thomas's tearful and apprehensive widowed mother, the family traveled down the valley to Swansea by horse-drawn coach laden with whatever of their most-precious belongings they could manage to take with them.

In 1839, the railroads had not yet reached South Wales, though work was rapidly proceeding to complete Brunel's Great Western Railway from London to Bristol. From there, the Severn Tunnel would provide the rail link between Bristol and the towns of Newport, Swansea, and Cardiff, in Wales. Rail links between South Wales and Liverpool were non-existent; the Mid-Wales line, connecting Swansea to Shrewsbury did not open its first link until 1852; its final link was not completed until 1868, long after David had emigrated.

1

The sailing ship Roscius

To travel by stage coach on winding, poorly kept roads through the mountains and moorlands of Wales was unthinkable. In 1839, the quickest way to get to Liverpool from Swansea was to travel by ship. Although the transatlantic port of Bristol was much closer to Swansea, special circumstances made David choose Liverpool as the port from which to cross the Atlantic. To get to Liverpool, he chose the *Mountaineer*, a ship that David had read about in *The Cambrian*.

The Cambrian, the leading English-language Welsh newspaper of the time, published in Swansea, described the *Mountaineer* as "a most reliable vessel, possessing 140 horsepower." A ship's notice advertised the fares for the gallant little vessel's regular sailings, "weather permitting," to and from Liverpool and Swansea, via Milford Haven. Best cabins were 25 shillings, only a little less than the steerage fare to the United States or Canada ; horses were carried at 30 shillings each; four-wheel carriages cost 40 shillings; dogs at 5 shillings; pigs were carried at 2 shillings and 6 pence; lambs, at one shilling; and horned cattle at 12 shillings and 6 pence.

Though small and cramped, the ship had stewards aboard who could be hired by ladies and gentlemen for 2 shillings and 6 pence, with an additional one shilling and 6 pence for each child above seven years and for each servant. On the uneventful voyage around the Welsh coast, the Thomas family had traveled in a "best cabin," plain, but cozy enough compared to the rough shelters in steerage offered those who could not afford a cabin. Their accommodations were situated away from the smells and noises of the many animal pens on board. They were nevertheless glad to reach Liverpool without getting too sick.

At Swansea, while they were waiting to embark, sea captains and old sailors had told the children dreadful tales of shipwrecks off the Anglesey coast, up in far-off North Wales, almost within sight of Liverpool. (Twenty years later, the *Royal Charter* was to go down off Moelfre with the loss of 400 lives). They were unafraid. for the sturdy little *Mountaineer* seemed reliable enough. It had made the journey many, many times.

Despite high winds and storms so common in Cardigan and Liverpool Bays, the week-long journey from to Liverpool around the coast of Wales had been uneventful. The children, only a little sea-sick on the first leg to Milford Haven, had been delighted with the views of the magnificent Pembrokeshire coastline, with its rocky cliffs. They had been able to spot the grand sweep of Cardigan Bay, its little fishing villages sparkling in the Spring sunshine; and, further north, the dramatic landscape of distant Snowdonia, with its cloud-wreathed peaks.

The children were thrilled, too, by the sight of the forked mountain on the Llyn Peninsula called "Yr Eifl." Its peaks were faintly visible on the mainland as the little ship safely made her way round the flat, green isle of Anglesey, "the Mother of Wales," then through the notorious rocks known as the Skerries before their approach to the busy, bustling port of Liverpool.

At Liverpool, in spite of the wonderful views they had enjoyed, it was especially exciting for the children to go aboard such a splendid ship as the *Roscius* after their cramped journey from Swansea on the *Mountaineer*. Built by Brown and Bell of New York, at 1,009 tons, and named after a very successful actor of Classical Rome, the *Roscius* was considerably bigger than any other packet ship of her time, even bigger and faster than her three sister ships of the American Dramatic Line: the *Shakespeare* the *Siddons* and the *Sheridan*.

All four clippers, belonging to the E. K. Collins Company, of New York, were faster than any other ships possessed by both the American and British merchant fleets. Able to outrun anything in the navies of both countries, they had been built expressly for the Atlantic emigration route to replace the old, slow brigs that had been carrying passengers in great discomfort from Liverpool to New York for the past half century.

Liverpool was fast becoming one of the busiest and largest ports in the world. Its vast number of docks stretched for miles from the Pierhead, yet the tall, slender masts of the *Roscius*, only recently completed, towered above the rest in the veritable forest of ships' masts that lined the Liverpool Landing Stage. Her main mast towered 160 feet above the deck; her main yard was 75 feet long. The Thomas family could only imagine how splendid she would look with her immense spread of canvas unfurled as soon as she reached the sea channel outside the harbor to begin her ocean voyage to the United States.

Captained at the time by American Asa Eldridge, the *Roscius* was to have a most important influence on the design of future clipper ships. Her building costs had been enormous: almost 100, 000 pounds, far exceeding the cost of any previous packet. But her cabins were finished in the most expensive woods and were spacious and comfortable, with room for people to stand up and walk about. The Thomas family looked forward to the Atlantic crossing and to their new life in Pennsylvania.

Chapter Two

Developments at Ynyscedwyn Iron Works

David Thomas was born in 1794 at "Ty Llwyd," the family farm, situated on marginal land high above Bryn Coch, Cadoxton Parish, just up the valley from Neath, a burgeoning industrial town a few miles east of Swansea. Having to pay high rent for 80 acres of land that belonged to the Dyffryn Estate, his parents had to scrape and save to send him to school.

The only boy in the family, David was lucky enough to be first tutored at the nearby Alltwen School until he was nine years old. Speaking only Welsh at home, he then attended the Neath Academy, where he was among the few privileged children in the district to learn to speak, read and write English, a language still unknown to most of the farming and mining families in the area.

The Thomases belonged to a group of hard-working farm families who were experiencing a time of great hardship at this time in western Glamorganshire, South Wales. There had been a prolonged period of cold, wet, unproductive weather and low harvest yields. A future in farming was far too unreliable as a source of family income, and, like many of his fellow-countrymen, David saw a better future in industry. In his own words, he took no pleasure in farming and would much rather "any day see a steam engine than a plow." His parents managed to find the fees required for him to attend the academy at Neath and to support his apprenticeship at the Neath Abbey Iron Works.

The Industrial Revolution had come to South Wales early. Before the end of the 18th century, Swansea had become the chief copper producer of Britain, if not the world. The Seven Years War of 1756-1763, involving much of Europe's great powers, had accelerated the demand for domestic iron, a great deal of which was produced in southeast Wales. After the process of puddling, invented by Englishman Henry Cort in 1783, had ended the iron industry's reliance on charcoal, the bituminous or semi-bituminous coals of southeast Wales had provided an extremely valuable, readily available fuel for the proliferation of furnaces centered around Merthy Tydfil.

By 1827, the southeast Wales iron industry, led by industrial giants such as John Guest, Anthony Bacon, Richard Crawshay, and the Homfrays, was producing one half of all Britain's iron exports, much of it to the United States.

Farther West, in the Swansea Valley, only three miles from Cadoxton, the Neath Abbey Iron Works operated two cold blast furnaces next to the ruins of the ancient abbey. The works were owned by a Welsh Quaker named Price, who was one of the largest builders of mining machinery and Cornish pumping engines of that day. Price also owned extensive machine shops, and it was here, at the age of seventeen, that David had taken up his apprenticeship.

David had spent five years at the Neath Abbey Works acquiring his technical training. He devoted many of his leisure hours to the study of the workings of blast furnaces. His abilities as a hard-working leader and innovator had been quickly noted by Mr. Henry Taylor, the chief engineer, who had given him leave to visit Cornwall in 1817 for several months to erect a pumping engine. It was an invaluable experience for young David.

Ty Llwyd Farm, Bryncoch, near Neath

Upon David's return to Neath, both his abilities as a resourceful worker and his sober, steadfast character had soon caught the attention of Mr. Richard Parsons, the owner of the Ynyscedwyn Iron Works, at Ystradgynlais, a small mining community thirteen miles up the valley from Swansea. Thomas was there offered the stewardship, not only of the furnaces, but also of the company's coal and iron mines, a position he occupied for the next twenty-two years.

The Ynyscedwyn Iron Works had been in operation since 1720, though iron had been produced on the site on a small scale as early as 1612 and a furnace had been erected in 1628. When Parsons went bankrupt in 1817, the works were left in the receivership of a Swansea banker, and Thomas supplemented his income by selling coal and lime and by working for the Brecon Forest Tramroad at Castell Ddu, Defynog, further up the valley.

This tramroad had been built especially to supply limestone for the furnaces at Ynyscedwyn, which had been having difficulty using locally mined coal since the 1790's. But it was at the Iron Works, not on the tramroad at Defynog, where Thomas's revolutionary work with anthracite took place. According to his youngest son Samuel, speaking over sixty years later, the opportunity came when David considered the rich resources of the Swansea Valley and decided that the Almighty had not wasted his creative powers in putting these materials together for no purpose. "On that faith," stated Samuel, "he began his experiments."

The Ynyscedwyn works lay at the edge of one of the largest coal fields in the British Isles. The coal, however, was not fully exploited, for it contained such a low quantity of potential gas that it did not coke properly and was therefore considered useless for iron smelting. It was anthracite coal, difficult to burn and universally called stone coal, called in Welsh, *glo caled* (hard coal). The works had to bring in better-burning coal (or coke) from elsewhere in Wales, mostly by horseback. In the early part of the century, this was a slow and expensive business. Railroads had not yet arrived, and canals had to cope with enormous topographical difficulties in the steep-sided Welsh valleys.

In 1833, in *A Topographical Dictionary of Wales*, Samuel Lewis wrote of the current situation in industry in the Ystradgynlais district, on the borders of Brecon and Glamorgan. "The iron ore and limestone used in the works are procured in the parish," he stated, "but the stone coal being unfit for the purpose of smelting iron, a supply of their coal is obtained from mines in some of the neighboring parishes." Though fuel had to be brought in from these outlying areas, there was "...this bountiful supply of magnificent fuel [anthracite] lying under their very works."

Particularly interested in trying to find a way to use these plentiful supplies of anthracite coal to smelt iron in the Ystradgynlais district, David Thomas began his work with revolutionary methods almost as soon as he arrived at the Ynyscedwyn Works. According to Samuel's recollection, his father was convinced that when the fuel and ore lay together, as they did in the Swansea Valley, the fuel might be suitable for smelting the ore, provided the right process could be worked out. At Ynyscedwyn, therefore, David spent a great deal of his time trying to figure out this process.

The Ynyscedwyn Works contained the only blast furnaces erected on the bed of anthracite coal in west Wales, all the other Welsh furnaces being located further east where the bituminous or semi-bituminous coal was easier to mine and burned more easily. In fact, the largest ironworks in Britain were located in the southeast Wales coal field: at places such as Cyfarthfa, Pen y Darren, Blaenavon, all situated in the Merthyr district. At Dowlais, also in Merthyr, the iron works was on its way to become the largest in the world within few years. With the adjoining valleys, this area would later come to symbolize industrial South Wales.

Sometime in 1817 George Crane, a former nail maker, had arrived at Ystradgynlais from Bromsgrove, in the English Midlands to take up his position as works manager of the Ynyscedwyn complex. Having made large profits in his hardware business, and with considerable knowledge of the metal trade, he was appointed by the principal creditors of the works to try to make it financially successful. He succeeded admirably. In 1820, when he was thirty-six years old, he was appointed General Manager.

Three years later Crane took over and bought the lease from Fleming Gough, proprietor of the Ynyscedwyn Estate, to become part owner of the iron works, which possessed six furnaces. At that time, the village, mainly consisting of the iron workers' dwellings, was known simply as "Gough's Houses" (a local inn is still called "The Gough Arms").

Described by contemporaries as being very religiously inclined, "short in stature and temper," Crane ruled his works from his splendid house "Ty Coch" with almost feudal standards. He was an ardent Anglican, a strict Sabbatarian, and "a terror to drunkards." He was known to visit public houses on Sundays and "woe betide the men he found there." This severe religious attitude made him unpopular with his workers, many of whom skipped Sunday chapel services in favor of the great number of ale houses in the district.

According to many reports, Crane would pounce upon "some unsuspecting Baccanalians who might be cosily quenching their thirst after the previous Saturday night's carouse." Iron making, like coal mining, was indeed thirsty work, and Sunday offered the only time away from the back-breaking work in the furnaces, iron works, and coal mines.

On one occasion, Crane suspended work at the furnace to conduct a religious service in the carpenter's shop. Yet even Crane complained that stoppages of work on Sundays could seriously disrupt production at Ynyscedwyn, and he thought nothing of employing young children. Many of his Welsh workers, who referred to him as 'the little Englishman" or "the little man," were in awe of their English iron master, who was also a church warden and who apparently had little faith in their moral character. One of the skilled, sober and religious workers in whom he did possess great faith, however, was David Thomas, who soon became his superintendent of works, and who became known by the Welsh workers as "Dai Y Stiward" (David the Steward).

At the Ynyscedwyn Works, George Crane and his steward worked together to see if they could get anthracite to smelt iron. At first, under Crane's supervision, Thomas used anthracite along with coke at a ratio of 1:20 or 1:12; and though they sometimes did quite well with these mixtures, whenever anything had gone wrong with the furnace, the workmen had always blamed the fuel instead of the methods used in smelting.

Though his first experiments began in 1820, David later complained that because of these early failures in using percentages of anthracite, "the men became so prejudiced against it, that I had to give it up." By a stroke of luck, however, it took but one moment, ironically away from the works, for the realization to come that the fuel was not the problem.

According to the account later given by George Crane, all attempts to utilize experimental deduction to solve the problem were deemed unprofitable until one day, he suddenly was blessed with "intuitive inspiration." He was sitting in the library at his home, accompanied by David Thomas. The two men were discussing a pamphlet recently published by Mr. Neilson, manager of a Scottish Gas works, on the use of the hot blast in furnaces.

A few years before, at the Clyde Iron Works in Glasgow, Scotland, David Musket had discovered the use of blackband ironstone that contained a considerable proportion of coal and that could be smelted with difficulty. One of his partners was Walter Neilson, father of James, who had been carrying out his own experiments into the smelting of iron. In 1834, he produced the hot blast oven, an invention so successful that all the world's blast furnaces within a few years used the process.

Neilson's hot blast was produced by passing the current of air from the blowing engine into the furnace through a chamber made of wrought iron plates, somewhat similar to a boiler, set in brickwork and heated by a coal fire beneath it. It soon became apparent that the use of the hot blast raised the temperature in the furnace, brought about a more complete combination of the fuel, and lowered fuel consumption.

Higher temperatures in the blast also speeded up the smelting process, making possible much higher output from a given furnace in which fuel such as anthracite could be used. The increased temperature also allowed the sulphur to be taken out as calcium sulphate in the slag. Neilson took out his patent in 1828.

In the library of his grand house overlooking the iron works at Ynyscedwyn, George Crane was talking excitedly to Thomas; they had been watching the fire, burning slowly and not too effectively in the grate, fuelled by the local *glo caled*. According to his own recollections, David was using bellows to try to instill some warmth in the cold room. The thought suddenly came to him that perhaps a hot blast applied to the fire would make the anthracite "burn like pine."

According to an article in Swansea magazine, *The Red Dragon*, in 1883, it was Thomas who first suggested the idea to his employer Crane. Crane later claimed full credit for the idea. But in any case, the idea was born there and then of using hot blast in the furnaces at Ynyscedwyn to smelt iron with anthracite coal.

Consequently, as soon as suitable arrangements could be made, Thomas visited Glasgow in Scotland to see Neilson's hot blast technique in action and returned to Ynyscedwyn with a licence from Neilson to use it. He also returned with a mechanic to help him build the hot blast oven. George Crane, as owner of the works, received the credit and the patent for the idea. He took out his patent on 28th September, 1836.

At first, at Ynyscedwyn and other iron works in South Wales, there was much skepticism over the use of anthracite as fuel in the furnaces. The trouble in adopting the new process was that iron makers throughout Britain were very traditional in their methods. To them, the idea of using a hot blast seemed absurd. Furnaces were known to produce more iron in winter in colder temperatures than in the warmer temperature of summer. Not only that, but the winter iron was of a better quality. What the iron masters had not realized at the time was that it was the additional moisture in the summer air that had made the inferior iron, and not the higher temperatures.

In the Swansea Valley, many local iron masters were reluctant to believe "stone coal" could ever be used for smelting iron. Even as late as February, 1839, after David's successful experiments had demonstrated its use in iron smelting at Ynyscedwyn, an advertisement in *The Cambrian* for the sale of anthracite showed that there was still little idea of its potential in blast furnaces. The notice claimed that anthracite was "in general use for Dr. Arnott's stoves and for drying of malt." It was sold at 12 shillings and sixpence a ton solely for these purposes.

Many iron masters were slow to realize the enormous benefits that use of the hot blast would prove in those areas of the country where such coal as anthracite was readily available, especially since no effective system of rail transportation had come into being to bring in more combustible coal. One of those areas that was destined to benefit most was the Swansea Valley.

On February 5, 1837, David Thomas succeeded in smelting iron ore with anthracite as the only fuel. He had used ovens to heat the blast for the furnace. A revolution in the making of iron had begun. From that day on, David Thomas, George Crane, and the workers at Ynyscedwyn experienced no unexpected problems with using anthracite coal in their furnaces. Not only were they able to make good quality iron, but they produced iron far superior than any that had been made there previously, equal in quality to any iron made anywhere in the world.

Taking note of what was happening at Ynyscedwyn, Harry Scrivenor, a contemporary American historian, wrote: "Mr. Crane's works are situated on the anthracite formation [in Southwest Wales]; his attention has been for many years directed to its application for smelting purposes, but without success, until the idea occurred to him that a heated blast, upon the principle of Mr. Neilson's patent, might, by its greater power, enable him to complete the combustion of this peculiar coal."

Scrivenor also made this interesting and prescient comment: "Although the principal advantage of this discovery [the hot blast] is at present confined to

Scotland, it may, before many years have elapsed, exercise a material influence on the manufacture of iron both in France and America." Strangely enough, he doesn't mention the advantages to South Wales that had already been demonstrated and to which he had earlier referred. He gives no credit to David Thomas, and he does not mention the many years of experimentation that had already taken place at the Ynyscedwyn Works under Thomas's stewardship.

An article in *The Cambrian* on February 9, 1839 drew attention to the work being done Ystradgynlais: "It is only one year and a half since Mr. George Crane of the Ynyscedwyn Foundry, near Swansea, conceived the idea that the introduction of a current of warm air would remedy this inconvenience" it stated. "The question was of double importance to that gentleman as his furnace was situated in the anthracite district, whereas he was obliged to use coal which had to be transported some distance." According to the article, the first experiment, fueled with anthracite only, conducted at Ynyscedwyn in February, 1837 had succeeded admirably.

The report then listed two advantages of using anthracite in the refining of iron: "It has brought into use a combustible mineral found in the neighborhood, cheaper than bituminous coal, and consequently much less expensive than coke, and of which a much smaller quantity is required; and the quality of iron has been sensibly improved by the use of it."

The Cambrian continued to state that anthracite found in many parts of France did not have the identical properties of that of Wales which were so necessary for the manufacture of quality iron. "The same effect" it noted, "has hitherto been unattainable in France." In the United States, that time dependent upon Europe, particularly upon South Wales for most of its iron, stated the paper, many prominent iron masters were taking notice. French anthracite may not have worked in the new furnaces, but in another part of the world where there were ample supplies of anthracite, such as Pennsylvania, surely it would be perfectly suitable.

In the meantime, because of David's recent successful experiments, immediate continued prosperity and social progress was forecast for Britain in general, but particularly for southwest Wales, including the Swansea Valley. On June 29, 1838, it was reported in the newspapers that there had been a meeting of the anthracite proprietors at Swansea to form an association, the object of which was to demonstrate the applicability of anthracite coal "to those purposes to which it had been lately applied" [the manufacture of iron].

The committee was duly appointed, including the Marquis of Bute (who owned coal mines, canals and docks in South Wales and whose splendid family edifice occupied the site of Cardiff Castle) and David's employer, George Crane, owner of the Ynyscedwyn Iron works. The same day's papers reported a meeting at Liverpool of the Polytechnic Society that discussed the iron trade in Great Britain.

At the Swansea conference, referring to the recent discovery at Ynyscedwyn concerning the use of anthracite in iron-smelting furnaces, credited to Crane, Mr. Johnson reported, "It is difficult for anyone not acquainted with the vast abundance of this material, and often in situations where no other description of fuel is to be found in proximity to the ore, to conceive the vast accession to our national resources that must result from its successful application to the manufacture of iron."

Already, according to Mr. Johnson in his address, great changes had been recently taking place in many areas of South Wales. For example, the state of education was improving very much in the neighborhood of Merthyr; a very great proportion of the young men could read and many of them could write. The members of the temperance societies were very numerous, he continued, and also the Odd Fellows, members of which fraternities delight in walking as often as possible in public processions, on which occasions they appear "...quite as respectable as we see them on festival days in England."

"In the houses of the workmen, said Mr. Johnson, "there was a marked improvement as of late. "Most of them," he stated, "had good oak chests of drawers, bright as silver; cupboards, with a display of fancy china cups and glasses; and some of the younger women had a veneered work box; and all these little things display an attention to the lesser comforts and luxuries of life, of which, a few years ago, they had no idea.

"On the whole," Johnson continued, "I should say that there is a decided improvement in the general condition and circumstances of our workmen, but you must bear in mind that these are very flourishing times." In West Glamorgan, but three years ago, according to Mr. Johnson, there had been only a few small works whose produce was "comparatively trifling," but recent discoveries had created quite a new era in the history of the iron trade.

Mr. Johnson then went on to mention George Crane's discovery, that had added "to the valuable resources of this kingdom, for the purposes of the iron trade, a district 60 to 70 miles long, by 6 to 8 miles broad, abounding with the anthracite or carbon coal, lime and limestone etc." The district to which he referred was the Swansea Valley, in the heart of which lay the village of Ystradgynlais and the iron works at Ynyscedwyn.

The result of using the hot blast to smelt iron ore with anthracite coal was instant and far-reaching: it not only opened up the West Wales anthracite coal field but also had dramatic results in the manufacture of iron in the United States. Here, according to one author, the owners of the great anthracite coal measures were "watching like cats at mice-holes for any break in the cloud which seemed to hang over their fortunes." They were sure that their prodigious supplies of hard coal could be used as blast furnace fuel if only they could unlock the secrets of using it.

In 1838 the *London Mining Journal* brought to the American iron manufacturers the welcome news of the success at Ynyscedwyn. The news was repeated in the *Journal* of the Franklin Institute, and it was in the United States where the greatest benefits of the work of David Thomas were to be realized. There was a huge anthracite coal field in Eastern Pennsylvania waiting to be exploited, one of the world's largest, with readily accessible ores and limestone. All that was missing was someone such as David Thomas to show how to unlock its enormous potential.

Chapter Three

Iron Rails and Iron Ships

During the middle years of the 1830's, the manufacture of iron ships to travel the oceans and iron rails to cross the continents were beginning to transform the world. In the United States, there was a frantic race to be in the lead in both enterprises. David Thomas's arrival in 1839 and the part he was to play in the manufacture of iron couldn't have come at a better time.

During the time of David's early experiments at Ynyscedwyn, railroads had been making steady progress in Britain. As early as 1676 timber rails had been used in Northeastern England to support horse-drawn carts on rollers. In the same area, iron rails had been introduced at Whitehaven in 1737. The pace of progress quickened rapidly after Richard Trevithick had carried passengers on Christmas Eve, 1801 at a speed of 9 miles an hour in a steam carriage at Camborne, in Cornwall.

As Trevithick's primitive locomotive had run out of steam going up hill, a more effective locomotive was needed to run on iron rails. Mr. Samuel Humfray, owner of the Merthyr Iron Works, suggested that Cornishman Trevithick build an improved steam locomotive for the nine-mile track to Navigation House, Abercynon. In 1804 Trevithick demonstrated his unique steam-driven locomotive at Pen y Darren, in the Merthyr district, though the idea of carrying passengers was then still considered a novelty, especially since the iron rails were not safe enough to hold the weight of loaded carriages.

At Pen y Darren, Trevithick tested his steam locomotive on the horse-drawn tramroad (a plateway completed in 1802) that by-passed the numerous locks on the Glamorganshire Canal linking Merthyr to Cardiff. The earliest steam locomotive in the world, it was a four-wheeled tramway locomotive that hauled a five-wagon load of ten tons of iron and 70 persons at a speed of five miles an hour, for a distance of nine miles [some sources state 20 tons]. Though the track proved too brittle and not developed enough for effective use, a new, exciting phase in the history of transportation was soon to begin.

An article of Friday, Feb 24, 1804 in the Swansea newspaper referred to "the long-expected trial of Mr. Trevithick's newly-invented steam engine [which the inventor named *Catch-Me-Who-Can*] to draw and work carriages of all descriptions on various kinds of roads." The successful test had taken place on

February 21. It drew forth the prescient comment: "It is not doubted but that the number of horses in the kingdom will be very considerably reduced, and the machine, in the hands of the present proprietors, will be made use of in a thousand instances never yet thought of for an engine."

In 1807 fee-paying passengers were taken in carriages on the horse-drawn railroad from Mumbles to Swansea, a line generally recognized as the world's first passenger-carrying railroad, originally designed in 1804 to carry ore from the mines at Clyne to the docks. But the innovation of using horse-drawn passenger carriages to run on rails was not to last. Trevithick's invention changed all that.

Improvements in steam locomotion had come rapidly after Trevithick's initial demonstration at Pen y Darren. The most dramatic break-through came when inventor William Hedley came up with his "Puffing Billy," an improved steam engine that carried passengers safely by relying on friction between the wheels and the rails, thus dispensing with the need for a toothed rack rail that had been used earlier.

In 1823, the great pioneer railroad engineer George Stephenson built a rail line between Stockton to Darlington, in Yorkshire, the first public railroad in the world to use locomotive traction and the first built to carry both freight and passengers. Throughout Britain, however, much opposition came from the landed gentry, who expressed great fears that the coming of such railways would despoil the countryside, cheapen land values and scare farm animals.

In London, a parliamentary committee denounced George Stephenson's proposals for a Liverpool-Manchester railway, calling it "the most absurd scheme that ever entered into the hand of man to conceive." A meeting of religious leaders in Manchester made a public statement that the locomotive " is in direct opposition both to the law of God and to the most enduring interests of society."

Stephenson was unfazed by these arguments. He went ahead with his plans. The Liverpool and Manchester Railway opened in 1830, utilizing locomotives such as Stephenson's Rocket that had proven superior to all others in a contest held by the railroad a year earlier. The success of this railroad opened up the world to the new means of transportation, so that by the end of the year 1830 the railroad era can said to have really begun.

Stephenson was then commissioned to build a railway between the cities of York and Leeds, and in 1839 this became part of the great inland route between York and London. Engines such as the *Rocket* demonstrated the feasibility of using steam as a power source; it remained the primary source of propulsion for the world's railroads for over a century.

In the United States, with its vastly greater distances between towns, and with the idea of the "extended republic" enshrined in the Constitution, interest in railroads occurred practically simultaneously to that in Britain. The early 19th century saw many horse-drawn tramways in operation; one, perhaps the first in the U.S., was used to carry granite from the quarries at Quincy and Charleston to build the Bunker Hill Monument in Boston, Massachusetts.

As early as 1813, Welsh-American Oliver Evans, who had pioneered many improvements in milling techniques along the Brandywine River in Delaware, proposed a railroad to link Philadelphia and New York City. In Hoboken, New Jersey, in 1825, inventor John Stevens built the first locomotive to run on rails in the United States, running it in a circle in the grounds of his home.

Stevens also built the *Phoenix*, a sea-going steamboat, and helped charter the Camden and Amboy Railway Company in 1830. In the meantime, Josiah White had constructed nine miles of track to take coal from Mauch Chunk to the Lehigh River, where it was loaded on boats for the journey to eastern markets.

News of the success of the Stockton and Darlington Railroad in England, followed by the Liverpool to Manchester line, spurred feverish activity across the Atlantic. At the same time Stevens was carrying out his experiments in Northern England, the Baltimore and Ohio Railroad Company received its charter. The line went into operation in Maryland in 1828, to be followed by rapid expansion that took it all the way out to the Ohio River at Wheeling, West Virginia.

In Baltimore, to demonstrate the potential of steam-powered rail transport, very necessary if any westward expansion was possible beyond the Appalachians, inventor Peter Cooper built the prototype locomotive *Tom Thumb* by fashioning steam tubes out of gun barrels. In 1831, the Boston and Worcester Railroad received its charter, and one-year later, the New Castle - Frenchtown Railroad opened for business. Practically astride the Mason-Dixon Line, it was to prove invaluable in providing links between the American North and the South. In Massachusetts, eight years later, a steam railroad was built to connect Springfield and Worcester.

At that time, because of the poor state of its own iron industry, America's fledgling railroad industry had to rely on expensive British imports of iron rails. In fact, when proposals had been submitted for the furnishing of rails for the Columbia and Philadelphia Railroad in 1831, there were none at all for American iron. The whole quantity was subsequently purchased in Britain, the great majority being produced in iron works in South East Wales, notably at Dowlais, Merthyr Tydfil. In fact, all the early railroads in the United States relied on the "Dowlais Rail."

Mr. Solomon Roberts, an inspector of rails, visited Ynyscedwyn on one of his visits to South Wales to see what was happening in the smelting of iron that was causing such a stir. Roberts was a nephew of Josiah White, manager of the Lehigh Coal and Navigation Company, where he been conducting experiments with the manufacture of iron rails as early as 1826. On account of the expense of bringing in suitable fuel, the work had been abandoned.

In a desperate attempt to remedy the situation, the company had been encouraging experimentation with anthracite, abundant in the area; and by 1834 it is reported as having supplied a local dealer with 1000 tons of that coal to be used exclusively in experiments in smelting iron ore. Solomon Roberts had been in Wales purchasing railway equipment at Dowlais Iron Works when news of the breakthrough at Ynyscedwyn reached him. Consequently, he paid a visit to the Swansea Valley to George Crane's works to acquaint himself with his methods.

Very favorably impressed with what he found at Ynyscedwyn, especially with Thomas's success in using a hot blast to smelt iron ore with anthracite, Roberts returned to Pennsylvania. He recommended that one of Crane's associates be employed by his own company, preferably the superintendent David Thomas, if he could be persuaded to emigrate. The company put forward their offer. It was a difficult decision for the Welshman.

Married to Elizabeth Hopkins of a nearby farm, and the father of sons John, David, and Samuel, and daughters Jane and Gwenllian, David was already 45 years old. Highly respected at the iron works, in the close-knit Welsh community of Ystradgynlais, and at Maes yr Haf Chapel, Neath, where his deceased father had been a church warden, he enjoyed a comfortable home and an interesting, fulfilling career. At Ynyscedwyn there seemed to be good prospects for continued employment. Despite this promising future in South Wales, the very attractive offer from the newly-formed Lehigh Crane Iron Company in Pennsylvania was simply too good for David to turn down.

A major contributing factor in David's decision may have been that George Crane, who was unmarried, had been experiencing some financial difficulties. On a business trip, he had met a young Irishman, Patrick Moir, who had just returned from Canada. Crane was impressed with the young man and invited him to marry his fiancee (who was still in Canada) and to set up residence at Tycoch. Moir's father then invested a considerable amount of money in the Iron Works, which were to become the property of Patrick upon Crane's death. Crane then adopted Moir, who became known as Moir-Crane. For reasons we can only guess at, the prospect that the Ynyscedwyn Iron Works would be inherited by Patrick Moir-Crane did not appeal to David Thomas.

Future events bore out the wisdom of David's decision to leave Ynyscedwyn. Not only was he to become enormously successful in Pennsylvania, where he would become known as "the father of the anthracite iron industry" but the death of George Crane only seven years after David's departure took away from Ynyscedwyn its prime impetus. According to Roger Thomas, who knew both men, Patrick Moir -Crane did not have the adventurous spirit of his adoptive father and had left the area "to a place unknown to us" without achieving anything of note at the Iron Works. He left behind a magnificent house, *Maes y Dderwen* later destroyed by fire, but little else "except a few cairns," to show that he had ever been at Ynyscedwyn.

Chapter Four

The Early Iron Industry in Pennsylvania

Before David came to the United States, the ample supplies of iron ores and the abundant coal of the anthracite region of Eastern Pennsylvania had not been utilized to any appreciable effect. They were all-too-often incapable of fusion, the ores had been of little use, and up to 1840, the iron produced in the area was comparatively small in quantity and extremely expensive. Consequently, the great majority of American iron came from abroad.

At the time when American railroad pioneers were busy planning new enterprises, they had to pay enormous sums for imported iron. In Pennsylvania alone, over 80,000 tons of iron were imported annually, and of these, 49,000 tons were of railroad iron from Great Britain, the bulk coming from South Wales.

This was a situation termed deplorable by historians such as Scrivenor, who saw the situation as one that "ought to cease forever." "Let us hope," he wrote, "that with this new power [the combination of ore and fuel]...we shall rescue ourselves hereafter from such a costly humiliation. We owe it to ourselves not thus to throw away the bounties of Providence, which in these very materials has blessed us with a profusion wholly unknown elsewhere. Pennsylvania has five times as much coal and iron as the country [Britain] to which we pay annually eight or ten millions of dollars for iron."

Scrivenor continued: "The anthracite masses of Pennsylvania are six or eight times as large as those of South Wales. With these resources you could have abundant employment, if you could only supply the present wants of the country, for which we are now dependent on foreigners. But the sphere of demand is every day widening for the consumption of iron."

"The time has come," said Scrivenor, "when nothing but iron roads will satisfy the importance of travelers and the competitions of trade. The time is approaching when iron ships will supplant these heavy, short-lived and inflammable structure of wood." The American historian was right: the age of the iron roads and the iron ships had already arrived.

Anthracite coal had been discovered in Pennsylvania, Rhode Island and Massachusetts about 1760, but only in Pennsylvania had the mining of the fuel been successfully carried out. It was slow finding acceptance as a useful source of energy. Soon after its discovery in the Wyoming Valley, a sample of the coal was taken to London in 1766 to be presented to Thomas and Richard Penn by Joseph Tilghman of Philadelphia, who had explored the region with a Colonel Francis. At the time, however, on both sides of the Atlantic the coal was regarded as little more than a curiosity, of no use in industry.

Some time in 1791, near present-day Scranton, about ninety miles northwest of Philadelphia, Philip Ginder was trying to extinguish his fire while out hunting on a hillside at Mauch Chunk (now called Jim Thorpe). He was astonished to find that certain black stones continued to burn. The "stones" were pieces of anthracite, part of the extensive deposits near present-day Summit Hill.

The fuel burned steadily enough once ignited, but because there were still great difficulties in getting it started, most of it was thrown away as useless for any purpose except to be used as gravel in footpaths. Despite Ginder's initial excitement, the huge coal field lay practically ignored; its potential unrealized.

In 1800, a wagon load of anthracite was taken by William Morris from Port Carbon to Philadelphia, but it was quickly returned because no -one would accept it. In 1812, Colonel George Schoemaker of Pottsville took nine wagons of coal from Centerville to Philadelphia but managed to sell only two loads with great difficulty. He had to give the other seven loads away. Many people in the city regarded him as an imposter who had tried to sell stone to the public as coal. But the slow-burning stone coal had already been used in stoves and grates as fuel.

In Philadelphia in 1804, the indefatigable Welsh-American inventor Oliver Evans had patented a "luminous grated stove" that could use anthracite or "mineral" coal, and Dr Thomas C. James is on record as being one of the first to use anthracite coal habitually to warm his house. In 1808, Judge Fell of Wilkes Barre, near Scranton, was also successful in using anthracite in a domestic grate.

The late Welsh-American historian Ellis Roberts tells of Judge Jesse Fell's success in burning anthracite coal in an open grate without having to apply a forced draft. He also tells of the experiments of Oliver Evans as well as those of the Smith brothers of Wilkes Barre, who shipped anthracite as domestic fuel to New York City in the early part of the century. These few attempts may have been the first to use the new fuel for domestic purposes in a grate in the United States or in any other country, as it was not used in Wales this way until 1813.

In 1828, a stove was perfected in Philadelphia by Williamson and Paynter, in which anthracite could be burned as well as charcoal. But though anthracite was finding its way into domestic fireplaces, it did not solve the major problem of finding a cheap, readily available fuel to smelt iron ore in sufficient quantities to be profitable in industry. The developments in railroads meant that this was where it was needed most.

Ample supplies of anthracite, especially in Pennsylvania, meant that there were continual efforts to exploit its potential. After Ginder's discovery, Joseph White and Erskine Hazard, who had been operating a wire mill at Schuylkill River Falls, decided to move their operations to exploit the new resources; they formed the Lehigh Coal and Navigation Company and constructed a canal, the Delaware and Hudson Canal. By 1824, this had been completed to a length of 124 miles expressly to carry the "stone coal" from the Wyoming Valley to the eastern markets where there were many small-scale iron works.

The first iron works in Pennsylvania seems to have been established in 1717, two years before the death of William Penn. This was a bloomary forge on Manatawny Creek above Pottstown, known as Pool Forge. The first actual furnace seems to have been the one at Colebrookdale, in Berks County, where David Jones, an immigrant from Wales, had settled in Caernarvon Township in 1735 and had become prominent as an iron master, making Berks County an important center of the industry. The nearby Phoenixville Iron Company began in 1790, and there was a rolling mill established at Coatesville, in the same area of eastern Pennsylvania, in 1810.

Despite these early attempts, before the arrival of David Thomas, the manufacture of iron in the whole country was, with relatively few exceptions, basically in the same technical state it had been when the first iron works were built at Saugus, in Massachusetts, in the late 17th Century. These had used charcoal and water-powered bellows to deliver a cold, low-pressure blast to produce small quantities of high priced, poor-quality iron suitable only for agricultural and mechanical implements.

Over a century later, the chief source of fuel for American blast furnaces was still charcoal, but in Pennsylvania as in Britain, supplies were being rapidly exhausted. In addition, problems of low production, poor quality iron, and that of finding the correct mixture of furnace size, blast pressure and temperature caused iron production to be abandoned in many areas. It was still cheaper for Americans to buy supplies from Great Britain.

The vast reserves of fuel and ore readily available, however, had led many to continue their experiments with anthracite, though it is not clear where it was first used for smelting iron in the United States. It is known that as early as 1815 the fuel had been mixed with charcoal in a furnace at Lanaconing, in Maryland. It was here also that Welsh immigrant, David Hopkins, joined by other Welsh ironworkers in 1837, built the most advanced furnace in the United States at the time.

Due to an economic recession, its remoteness from the eastern seaboard markets, and other factors including difficulties of operation, the Lanaconing furnace did not become the hoped-for commercial success. Some ten years previously, the Lehigh Coal and Navigation Company had built a small furnace at Mauch Chunk, but it also had proved unprofitable, though as we have seen, the company's interest in using anthracite continued.

A patent for smelting iron ore with anthracite was granted to Dr. F.W.

Geissenheimer of New York in December 1833 (some sources list him as Dr. Geissenhainer). Anticipating the work of David Thomas, the American inventor had used the hot air blast invented a few years earlier by Neilson, but despite some initial successes in producing iron, the results proved to be short-lived, the furnaces having broken down after only two months in operation. Granted a patent in 1831, the Reverend Dr. Geissenheimer died in 1838; his pioneering work did not lead to the expansion of the industry. His patent was bought out by the enterprising George Crane in 1838, after he and Thomas had been successful at their own iron works at Ynyscedwyn.

It didn't seem right to U.S iron masters that the patent for smelting iron with anthracite had been granted to an Englishman (George Crane) especially since there had been many other experiments in their own country in smelting iron with anthracite. In 1836, some of these were undertaken by John Pitt at Mannheim Furnace at Cressina, Schuylkill County, Pennsylvania ; and though Pitt seemed satisfied that the scheme was practicable, an end of the experiment came when thawing ice flooded the whole works. It did not stay in operation for any length of time despite its initial success at producing a considerable amount of pig iron of good quality.

Also in 1837, there were also experiments using high percentages of anthracite and the hot blast at the old furnace of the Lehigh Coal and Navigation Company at Mauch Chunk, but something vital was missing, and the company could not discover what the problems were. White and Hazard's attempts also ended in failure.

In 1838, Mr. B. B. Howell, secretary of the American Iron Trade Committee, claimed to have succeeded in converting iron ore to malleable iron with anthracite exclusively at his works in New Jersey. He claimed to have made bar iron as good as that of any of his neighbors and stated that he was able to turn it into nails "without even letting it first cool." Yet Howell, like so many of the early pioneers, was unable to turn his small-scale foundry into a profitable, commercial enterprise. Desperate to make the United States independent of Britain in this important industry, others continued the search.

The claims to have been the first to succeed continued to proliferate on both sides of the Atlantic. In 1840, in a dispute over patent rights, Jesse B. Quinby said that he was the first person in the United States to use anthracite in smelting iron. He testified that he had been successful at a small furnace in Harford, Maryland with anthracite mixed with charcoal as early as 1815.

In addition to these early attempts, in the fall of 1840, William Henry, another American iron master, no doubt having heard of the success at Ynyscedwyn two years before, and encouraged by what David had achieved at Pottsville for Lyman, built an anthracite furnace on the Lackawanna River in the area now known as Scranton, Pennsylvania.

Henry had great problems in getting the necessary fire-brick, blast machinery, and hot blast apparatus from American manufacturers. It was not until the following year that he could attempt the first blast, and it ended in total failure. Welsh iron worker John F. Davis, who worked at one of the anthracite furnaces in the Danville area finally was able to put the Lackawanna Ironworks in order in 1842, but this was two years after David Thomas had been successful at his furnace in Catasauqua.

Until the arrival of Thomas, therefore, in none of these early attempts was there any sustained success. As a result, apart from the experimental furnaces mentioned above, up to the year 1840, the iron industry in the Lehigh Valley was mostly confined to a few charcoal furnaces and one rolling mill. After news of the astonishing results of the experiments of Crane and Thomas at Ynyscedwyn reached Pennsylvania, the advantages of using the new methods could not be ignored.

It was necessary for someone to take action. In July, 1838, the board of directors of the Lehigh Coal and Navigation Company passed a resolution "to give in fee simple" to any company who would expend the sum of $30,000 to establish works to smelt iron with anthracite all the water power of any one of its dams between Allentown and Parryville, "except that necessary for the operation of the canal."

The Lehigh Crane Iron Company took up the challenge, becoming organized the same year (though it was named after George Crane, the patent holder, he took no part in its operations nor did he invest in it). The newly-formed company, working to a strict deadline, and upon the advice of Solomon Roberts, accepted the proposal by authorizing its representative, Erskine Hazard to go to Ynyscedwyn to try to entice David Thomas. George Crane took Erskine to Castell Ddu, the terminus of the Brecon Forest Tramroad, where David had been working as a manager in addition to his duties at Ynyscedwyn.

David finally agreed to the terms of the attractive contract to come to the United States "... for a period of five years to manage the setting up of a furnace on or near the River Lehigh to smelt iron with anthracite, and to generally use his best knowledge and services for the good of the company." According to George Crane, his decision was one that would lead to the Welsh iron master's becoming "the greatest benefactor to Pennsylvania that ever lived

Despite David's relatively advanced age, and his highly regarded status in the community, at Maes yr Haf Chapel, and at the iron works, five years didn't seem too long. The family could always return to Wales if things didn't work out; his ample salary would enable him to send enough money home to keep his family in comfort as well as enough to send home to his widowed mother. George Crane, his employer, was all for the move and actively encouraged it; after all, it could furnish him the opportunity to have his patent honored in America and his name made famous throughout the industrial world.

The agreement with the Lehigh Company was very tempting: it offered to pay the expenses of the Thomas' family from Wales and to furnish them with

A copy of the contract that took David to America

a house and coal for fuel. It offered to pay a salary at the rate of two hundred pounds sterling a year until the first furnace on the Lehigh "...is got into blast with anthracite coal and making good iron; and after that at the rate of two hundred and fifty pounds sterling a year until a second furnace is put into operation successfully, when fifty pounds sterling shall be added to his annual salary, and so fifty pounds sterling per annum additional for each additional furnace with may be put into operation under his management."

In addition to these generous terms, should Thomas fail in his attempts to produce quality iron from anthracite, then the company was to pay him a sum equivalent to the expense of removing himself and family from the Lehigh Valley to their present residence in Wales.

On March 9, 1839 an article in *The Cambrian* stated that the Brecon Forest Tramroad Company, "in consequence of their present manager, Mr. David Thomas, intending to go to America, request all persons having any demands on the firm, to send their accounts to Mr. Llewelyn Jeffreys, at Castell du Wharf, Defynog, near Trecastle." David, we remember, had earlier moved temporarily to Defynog to supervise the building of the tramway from there to Ynyscedwyn. It was as superintendent of the Ynyscedwyn Iron Works, however, that he was invited to move to Pennsylvania, not as manager of the tramway.

A notice appeared in the same newspaper on May 25th of that year of an auction to be held at the Castle Inn, Neath. For sale were seven newly-erected cottages or dwelling houses "now in the possession of Mr. David Thomas and his under tenants." While there may have been many men named David Thomas in the Neath area, it seems very likely that this was our David Thomas anxious to get rid of his property before sailing for America. This hunch is confirmed by a letter of George Crane in which he stated he didn't like the idea of David disposing of his property in Wales, for it seemed that as if he were separating himself permanently from his native country.

On July 6, 1839, *The Cambrian* advertised for a person to contract for the working of iron mine; it also asked for a person competent to undertake the management and working department of a blast furnace at the Ynyscedwyn Iron Works. David Thomas and his family had sailed from Swansea in May.

Chapter Five

To Allentown: the Atlantic Crossing

In April, 1839, just before leaving Wales for good, though he wasn't aware at the time that he would never be returning, David Thomas was honored by the presentation of a silver medal from members of the Total Abstinence Society of Devynock (Defynog). The medal was given to him as a token of sincere respect for him as "a most exemplary member of the society" and for "his indefatigable exertions to further its desirable objects and promote the moral and religious improvement of the above district." One month later, the family was on its way to America.

Upon their safe arrival at Liverpool, the family had but a short time to look around this great northern city before they embarked on the *Roscius*. The size and bustle of the four major docks and the sheer bulk of the massive public buildings simply overwhelmed them, but so did the scenes of abject poverty and degradation in street after crowded street only a short distance away from the Pierhead.

This was the first time the Thomas family had seen colored people; they were astonished. David had been to the little town of Brecon, of course, north of Ystradgynlais; he had visited towns in Cornwall, in the southwest of England during his early years as an apprentice. The family had sailed from the largest port in Wales, at Swansea; David had even ventured as far as Cardiff, but these were very small towns compared to the port of Liverpool, then the second largest city in England, with a population fast approaching 300,000.

In the time that his family were allotted to look around and to do their last minute shopping before embarking upon the *Roscius*, they had enough time to see Abercrombie Square with its fine Georgian houses; the impressive public buildings, including the elegant Town Hall, with its fancy display of the city's regalia; the large commercial buildings facing Pier Head; the huge Albert Dock, then in the process of construction, with its granite warehouses and cast iron pilasters; and the impressive foundations of St. George's Hall, high on its plateau, showing all the signs that it was to become, when finished, one of the most magnificent municipal buildings of England.

The family lingered briefly at the infamous granite-columned Goree Piazza, the former offices of the slave trade before that nefarious practice had been abolished in the British Empire in 1834, only nine years before. The Piazza was now filled with offices of brokers, provision merchants, ships' chandlers, iron-mongers, fish merchants, tea and coffee importers, spice vendors, and various shipping companies.

In front of the Piazza's long colonnade, lines and lines of horse-drawn drays laden with produce from the farthest reaches of the Empire were waiting patiently to have their contents checked before being hauled away to distribution points that would send them to all parts of Britain.

Envelope of a letter from Wales to Allentown via "the first ship to America".

The sights, smells and sounds of this area of the dock-lands were overwhelming, but exciting too, for a family from a green, pastoral valley, and it was here that David and his wife made their last minute purchases, irresistibly drawn to the exotic foods and goods for sale. They couldn't help notice the crowds of poor Irish, many of them in rags and barefoot, waiting in long lines to buy their meager provisions, for steerage passengers on the Atlantic crossing had to provide their own food. It was pitiful to see so many in so such poverty being preyed upon by unscrupulous merchants.

But it was soon time to board ship and depart for America. After she had provisioned herself and put herself in trim, the *Roscius* cautiously left the landing stage, slipped out of the Waterloo Dock, and moved slowly up the wide Mersey estuary to begin her long voyage across the Atlantic.

The Thomas family, nervous but excited, stayed on deck to watch as the motley crowd of trinket peddlers, fruit merchants, clothes dealers, tailors, and pushers of all kinds of items pushed their way down the gangplank when ordered to leave. Before reluctantly getting off the ship, they tried to convince passengers to buy items they might need on the long voyage. David purchased some of the famous Everton toffees for his children.

The family was spellbound as their ship moved out from the vast, crowded docklands of Liverpool, furled her massive sails to glide majestically past the uninhabited Hilbre Islands off the Wirral Peninsular, with their vast flocks of wading birds. The ship then quickened her pace past the Point of Ayr, on the North Wales Coast, where the Afon Dyfrdwy (River Dee) finally emptied into the Irish Sea to end its long, winding journey from Llyn Tegid (Lake Bala) in the green, mist-shrouded Welsh hills.

The day was clear enough to see the magnificent outlines of Pen y Gogarth, known in English as "The Great Orme" that sheltered the tiny fishing village of Llandudno; followed by the massive headland of Penmaenmawr and the high, cloud-covered summit of Yr Wyddfa and his lofty companions in Snowdonia. Then, much relieved after the ship had cleared the dangerous rocks known as "The Skerries," the passengers could faintly make out the winking light on the rocks at South Stack, on Holy Island, Anglesey "the Mother of Wales," just before they lost sight of land altogether.

It was sad to be leaving everything they had ever known, but even as the faint, blue smudge that was Wales faded away on the horizon behind them, the family was in good spirits; they had heard so much about the New World. With good weather and favorable winds, they would be there in three weeks; it was an exciting prospect.

David was very ill during the last few days of the otherwise uneventful three-week voyage, confined to his cabin. The illness was a mysterious one, and neither his family nor the ship's crew could do anything to alleviate his fever. There was no doctor on board, but Elizabeth was a great comfort to him, constantly by his bedside. Feeding her husband with beef tea, she constantly reassured him that he would recover soon and fulfill the great promise expected of him by all in Wales.

America would be a great country to live in, she told David, trying to cheer him up and make him well again. She knew very little of the United States, only that she had heard that one part of it was originally intended to be called "New Wales", that lots of Native Indians — the descendants of Prince Madog — had been discovered somewhere out in the wilds who spoke the Welsh language; that everybody was happy and well-fed; and that anyone who wanted work could find it.

Despite her lack of formal education, Elizabeth also had been told that there had been some kind of Declaration of Independence, put together mainly by Welsh settlers? David himself had read some where that many of the signers were Welshmen, proud of their success in at last freeing themselves from English rule. At school, the children had also learned of Dr. Richard Price, honored more in the United States than in Britain for his ideas on political liberty.

In the last few weeks before sailing, David had been trying to get as much information about his new home as was possible in a small village in a South Wales valley. At school, he had learned of the exploits of famous Welshmen of the past such as Charles Morgan, the driving force behind Spain's great enterprise, the Missouri Company. His teachers had told him and his eager-eyed school mates of Morgan's explorations in the West, where lived the Mandans, the tribe of Welsh-speaking Indians, the story of whom so excited Elizabeth and the boys.

David told his family of the explorations of John Evans, from Waunfawr, in North Wales, who had not only found the Mandans, but he had also lived with them for six months. Evans's maps of the frontier were later used by Lewis and Clark on their epic journey to the Pacific. David also told them of the Welsh Baptists under John Miles, who had settled in New England, calling their new home Swanzey, after the port from which the family was sailing to Liverpool.

Of course, David told them of the state of Pennsylvania, an area that William Penn had originally wanted to name "New Wales" but which, his Welsh secretary demurring, he finally agreed to name after his father the Admiral, thus satisfying the wish of King Charles ll. This also nicely accommodated Penn's earlier desire that the territory should be named after the Welsh word "Pen" meaning "high" or "chief" affixed to the Latin for "woods." Pennsylvania would be a grand state in which to live.

Wasn't Philadelphia the city where Welsh was spoken in the streets"? Hadn't Thomas Wynn, from Caerwys, in Flintshire, helped William Penn lay out the design of those very streets? America wouldn't be so strange, after all, despite the horrible stories of the wild animals, vast woods and savage tribes to the West. At least there were no Chartists there, causing trouble wherever they went! Perhaps the family could attend Welsh chapel and speak their beloved language to their neighbors. Elizabeth knew no English; she had never needed it.

To travel on the *Roscius* proved to be a wise choice, even though the journey could have been made faster by one of the new steam ships. Technological advances in the late 18th and early 19th centuries, particularly the advent of the age of steam and the building of iron ships had brought about great changes in construction and propulsion. It may not have been until World War 1 that the deathblow finally came to sailing ships, especially since steamships needed such a great amount of fuel for long voyages, but a combination of steam and sail was utilized until the waning years of the nineteenth century.

Chapter Six

The Age of the Iron Steamship

In the extraordinary expansion of maritime industry, it is important to note that though anthracite played a major role in the fuelling of the new steamships, it played an even larger one in the use of iron for ship-building (in addition to the construction of railroads). Through the use or iron for shipbuilding, wooden sailing ships such as the magnificent *Roscius* were the last of their kind.

Half a century before the Thomas family sailed from Liverpool, at Coalbrookdale, in the English Midlands, industrial pioneer and iron manufacturer John Wilkinson conceived the revolutionary idea of building ships out of iron. In 1789, he completed his first such ship, the *Trial*, proving that a ship made of iron would float. In 1818 came the *Vulcan*, and in 1821 the *Aaron Mamby*, both built with iron hulls.

Experiments with these pioneering iron ships had proved successful, but for quite some time afterwards iron was used only to construct ice boats used to break up the ice on frozen rivers. Trials continued, however, and in March 1830, the aptly named *Ironsides*, built of iron, and the first sailing ship of that construction ever dispatched on a foreign voyage from Britain was reported by *The Cambrian* as having reached the Brazils.

In 1834, when a fierce storm in the north of England drove ashore many ships, only the iron-hulled *Garryowen* was able to re-float itself and proceed unscathed. Iron had proved itself graphically over wood as a material for building ships' hulls. It was quickly adopted by all the major shipyards in Europe and the United States (in 1852, the *Arabia*, the last Cunard ship to be built of wood, was already obsolete).

The period 1830 to 1885 is generally referred to as "the iron shipbuilding age" (it was replaced by the age of steel in the 1880's). The first iron steamboat in the United States was constructed in 1839 in Pittsburgh. There followed such a rapid progress in the use of iron for the construction of ships that one of the greatest revolutions of all time in shipbuilding took within a few years.

Iron not only dominated the output of British and American shipyards, but it soon became the main constructional material for ships throughout the world. In the late 1830's, it was pointed out in the American newspapers that

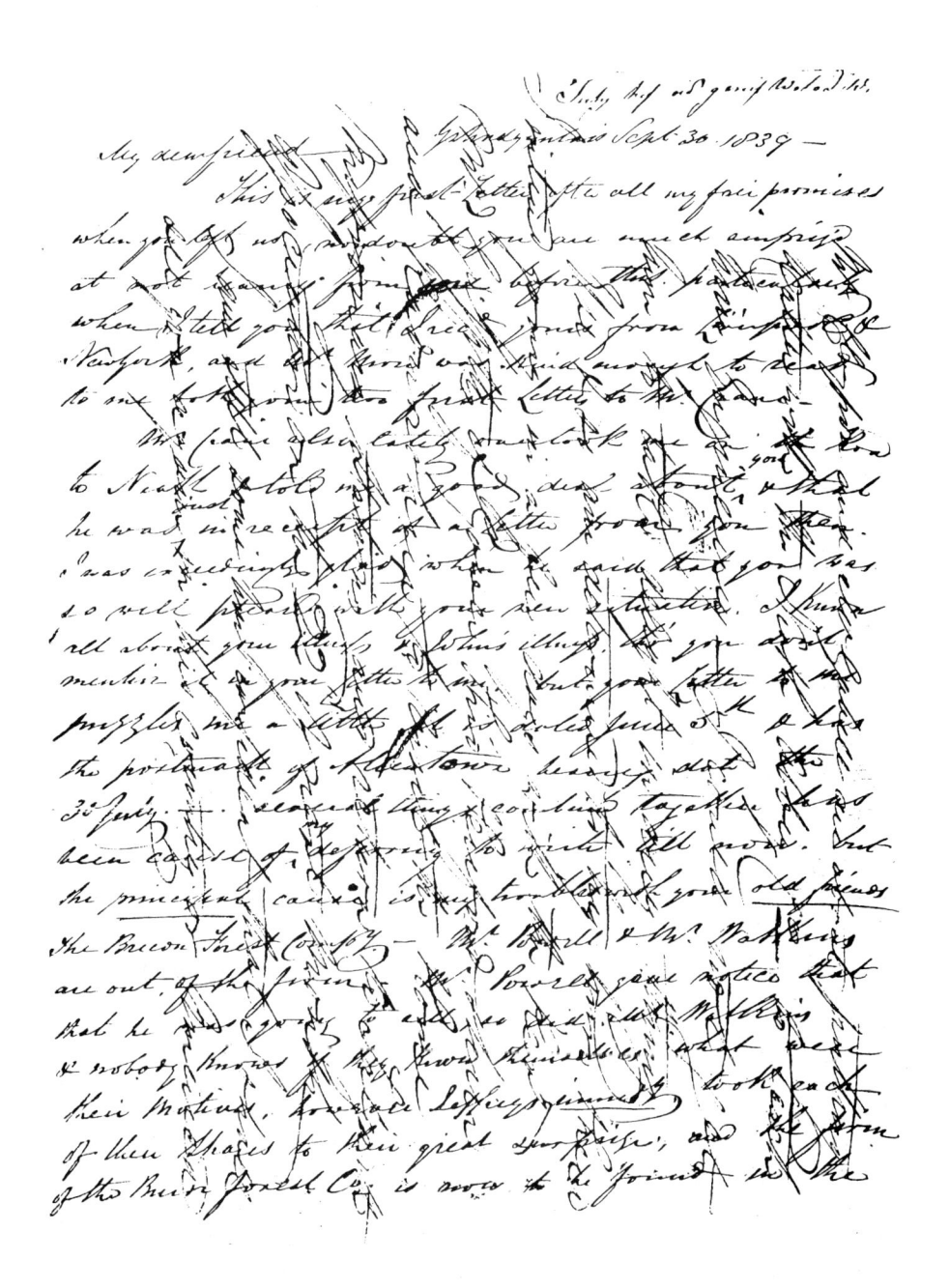

Sample page of an early letter in Welsh and English sent to David from Wales in September, 1839 before the post office reforms. It is written both vertically and horizontally to save paper.

iron vessels could be built as cheaply in the United States as abroad, and "the knowledge had attracted wide attention, with an increase in the orders for their construction speedily expected to follow." Iron produced at the furnaces built by David Thomas in the Lehigh Valley was to play a major role in this expansion of American ship-building.

The rapid expansion of the iron shipbuilding industry coincided, and in many instances was made possible by, the use of steam as a source of power, replacing countless centuries of sail. In 1803, American engineers had suggested to Napoleon that he could defeat the British fleet by the use of steam-powered ships. Luckily for the Royal Navy, the French dictator replied that he had no time to listen to such nonsense.

In the early 1820's steam packets were first employed to carry mail on the short voyage from Ireland to Britain; they were soon used to carry thousands of immigrants to the United States. The *Savannah*, a fully-rigged vessel built in New York, had crossed the Atlantic in 1819 using steam for 80 hours of its 25 days at sea. It carried engines and detachable paddle wheels in addition to its full complement of sail. Because of the general public's fear of steam engines in wooden vessels, especially outfitted for passenger comfort, the Savannah sailed with no passengers: it was later stripped of its engines and sold as a sailing packet. But the age of steam had begun.

As late as 1838, the British Association was told by a so-called expert that men might as well project a voyage to the moon as to attempt to employ steam across the stormy North Atlantic. Yet, along with sail, many ships had been using steam in such voyages for almost a quarter of a century. In 1827, using a combination of sail and steam, the *Curacao* crossed the Atlantic, soon to be followed by the *Royal William*.

In 1828, fearing it would be left behind, the British Royal Navy did what Napoleon had not dared to do: it commissioned its first steam vessel, the Lightning. By early 1839, there were 766 steam-propelled ships registered in Britain. One year before the Thomas family sailed from Liverpool, the first Atlantic crossing under steam alone was claimed by the *Sirius*. On April 8, 1839 departing from Cork, Ireland, using a paddle wheel, the *Sirius* arrived at New York in 18 days. A few hours later the *Great Western* arrived, a much newer and bigger vessel. She had departed Bristol 15 days earlier. The most famous of all the great steamships, she was designed by Isambard Brunel, who perhaps was the first to realize and exploit the value of iron in its construction.

The same year, the *British Queen* of 2400 tons inaugurated a regular Atlantic passenger service for the British and American Steam Navigation Company, carrying 500 passengers and 80 tons of cargo. She had taken a mere 16 hours on its maiden voyage from her berth at Greenock, near London, to Liverpool, a rate of speed described by The *Cambrian* as "seldom equaled by any vessel and perhaps never by anyone attempting a maiden trip."

The newspaper went on to praise the equipment and design of "this behemoth" as "a more splendid specimen of the progress of European arts and manufacture as had never provoked competition or elicited applause." There was wild enthusiasm at her arrival in Liverpool.

On March 30 of 1839, only two months before the Thomas family sailed, it was reported in British newspapers that the governments of the United States and Britain had entered into a contract for conveying the mails by large and powerful steamers from Liverpool to Halifax, and thence by steamers to Boston. The paper stated, "...and the mercantile interests would be gratified to learn that, instead of monthly communications, steamers would now be dispatched on the 1st and 15th of each month." On the new ships, there would be plenty of space available for passengers.

In weighing his decision as to which ship would best take his family to America, David must have been tempted by the notice in *The Cambrian* of January 12, 1839, stating that the finishing of the *Great Western* was almost complete, "with a saloon of 72 feet in length." The ship would be open for inspection before proceeding from the dry dock to Bristol on the evening's tide.

On May 25, the *Great Western* was reported as having sailed from Bristol with 107 passengers and about 9,000 letters and a very large number of newspapers. It reached New York on the last day in May, the fastest crossing ever made up until that time — over 3000 miles in thirteen days.

Later in the year, at a meeting of the Great Western Steamship Company at Bristol, it was stated that though the iron ship had run 35,000 nautical miles and encountered 36 days of heavy gales, her seams had required no caulking. When docked, she had not shown a single wrinkle in her copper. The company determined to build their second vessel of iron. In October, 1839, the *President* was built in London for the British and American Steamship Company. With a tonnage of 2500, with 90-foot paddle wheels, it was reported as being even bigger than the *British Queen*.

The same month that the Thomas family departed for America, there were additional notices in *The Cambrian* that arrangements had been made by the British and American merchants to dispatch regular lines of first-class sailing packets to Philadelphia, Baltimore, Boston, and New Orleans, two times a month; and to New York, four times.

The packets, of 700 to 1100 tons, could take a limited number of passengers who "are furnished with everything necessary for their comfort and convenience." In July, 1839, there appeared in Welsh newspapers notices of sailings to Philadelphia and New York from Cardiff of the American ship *Niagara*, of 600 tons.

Ship owners were anxious to dispel fears of the Atlantic crossing. An article in *The Cambrian* of January 19, 1839 stated that "Twenty years have now elapsed since the first establishment of the packet ships between Liverpool and New York. Only three have met with serious disaster until last week when three were wrecked." This is a remarkable record, since the pages of all the

British newspapers each day were filled with news of disasters both at sea and in coastal waters.

The first ship built specifically for liner service, the *Albion*, had been wrecked off the Irish coast with only eight survivors in 1822, the worst disaster in a quarter century. The site of the tragedy, off Old Head of Kinsale, was where the *Lusitania* was to meet her fate nearly one hundred years later, but for far different reasons.

The superior design of the packet ships helped them survive conditions that destroyed many other ships, but even then, a hurricane that swept the West coast of Britain in 1839 destroyed the *St. Andrew* and the *Pennsylvania* and severely damaged the *Lockwood*. The little coastal brig the Mountaineer that had taken the Thomases from Swansea to Liverpool, played a gallant part in the rescue of many passengers from the *St. Andrew* in the hurricane. The storm was so intense it had severely damaged Telford's 1826 masterpiece, the great Menai Straits suspension bridge, making land passage impossible between the island of Anglesey and the mainland.

In deciding which ship to take for the journey to North America, there was still the question of safety. Mechanical failures on some of the new steam ships meant many extra delays, and though speed was all-important for many emigrants, it was not the only consideration. Despite the great advances being rapidly made in all aspects of shipbuilding, for many fearful emigrants the reliability of the new steam ships was not yet fully proven. American and British newspapers reported countless steam boats blowing up in many rivers in both countries.

To travel by steamship was still considered by many to be a dangerous venture. The *Great Western* had made two or three voyages across the Atlantic in perfect safety. Sadly, however, in April, 1841, less than two years after the Thomas family left Liverpool, a letter from David's mother seems to lament the loss of the largest passenger liner afloat, the *President*, which disappeared with no trace somewhere in the North Atlantic. The ship was reported as missing with the loss of 136 lives on March 11, 1841 (April marked the death of the American President William Henry Harrison; it is not entirely clear whether David's mother was referring to the loss of the ship or the U.S. President).

A major factor that helped David make his decision to travel on the *Roscius* was that British ships were not built expressly for passenger service, and their captains were not known for their concern for their passengers. On the other hand, the American clippers were fast and reliable, commanded by experienced captains known for their concern for the welfare of their passengers.

The final decision for the Thomas family to travel on a sailing ship from Liverpool, rather than on one of the new, faster steamers now departing regularly from the much-closer port of Bristol, was made by Thomas Wood. A ship's agent at Liverpool, Wood wrote to David on May 6, 1839 informing him that he had gone ahead and booked three state rooms on the *Roscius*. They would sail on the 13th of the same month.

Mr. Wood's letter described the ship as decidedly the finest of all the packets sailing from Liverpool. If Wood himself were to go overseas, he stated, then he and his family would give the *Roscius* preference over any other vessel he had ever seen. He went on to describe the ship's construction, list the amenities available, and detail the price of the passage. The glowing testimonial clinched it for the Thomas family. It was Mr. Wood who had met them at Liverpool prior to their embarking.

The soundness of David Thomas's decision to travel all the way to Liverpool to take the *Roscius*, rather than the Great Western, the British Queen, or any other of the many other steam ships available, was borne out by the speed of the crossing. The ship took only 23 days to reach New York from Liverpool, an unprecedented run, for in bad weather the she had been known to take as long as 54 days on the same trip. Some ships of the same size had been taking as long as 60 days or more in winter or in stormy weather. The Roscius was only four days behind the *Great Western*, both having left England on the same day.

During the early years of the 19th century, fares on the Atlantic crossing were very expensive, but in February 1822, the Black Ball Line, one of the most popular of all the early packet lines, had reduced its eastbound fare to 35 guineas. Westbound fares soon dropped accordingly; the Liverpool Lines Company soon followed suit, dropping its fare to 30 guineas "wines included," and this rate seemed to be standard for the next ten years.

In 1834, because lots of passengers did not drink any liquor or spirits at all, Liverpool and London packet owners had agreed that wines and liquors were to be furnished by the steward upon request and not to be included in the regular fare. In 1838 the *Great Western* advertised a fare of $140.00, equivalent to 30 British guineas. This price not only included wine, but also provisions for its Atlantic fare. All the other sailing lines had to drop their prices to compete.

According to Wood's letter, the fares for the Thomas family were to be as follows: one room in ladies cabin for Mr and Mrs Thomas 73 pounds 10 shillings: two rooms adjoining the above for the two daughters, 73 pounds ten shillings; one room in gentleman's cabin for the boys, 36 pounds 15 shillings. Total cost to be 183 pounds and 15 shillings. Wines were included, as the New York packets, wrote Wood, made no difference when people are "tea totallers." The Thomases, of course, were not interested in the inclusion of wine, or of any alcoholic beverages.

Mr. Wood's letter goes on to state that the rate of passage was 35 guineas (35 pounds and 35 shillings) for all above twelve years of age, but that "the consignees of the buffet engage to take the two boys at half price and not to count the youngest." Wood then states that he had endeavored to put the younger daughter at half price, but the consignee refused — the captain being out of town. Upon his return, goes on Wood, he would battle the point with him, "if successfully, so much the better."

The Thomas family couldn't have been too concerned about the prices, for their passage was paid by the Lehigh Crane Company in Pennsylvania, and they were going first class, as the prices indicated. At that time, steerage was only 2-3 pounds a person, but this included no food and as many as four people shared a bunk.

Welsh passengers who traveled that way, and steerage passengers were in the majority, were advised to prepare oat bread, cheese, butter and meat beforehand in Wales. Anything else, they were told, they could buy in Liverpool, such as tea, treacle, flour and potatoes. They'd have to take turns with the other steerage passengers in cooking their food.

The Great Britain in Dry Dock, Bristol

In July 16, 1836 Welsh emigrant William Griffiths paid 4 pounds for the journey from Liverpool to Baltimore and an extra 30 shillings for food and "everything" from Baltimore to Pittsburgh. Unlike many thousands of others who traveled steerage and who had found it to be a veritable hell, Griffiths seemed to be quite satisfied with his journey. He wrote back to Wales that not only did he have a job at Pittsburgh, where he worked for 4 shillings and sixpence a day ("of your money"), and paid 9 shillings and six pence a week for food and washing, but that "this was [also] a good place for women to work."

Prices for the Atlantic passage were also low at this time because passengers were needed to fill ships that were bringing cotton, tobacco and timber to Britain from the United States and Canada. Welsh emigrants were warned, however, that the price of four pounds entitled them only to a place on the lower deck, described by one obviously biased writer as "the home of the Irish. Oh! hole of pity, darkness, barbarism, dirt, flies and stench." Crowded conditions certainly hastened the spread of disease aboard the emigrant ships, in which passenger comfort was one of the least concerns. On one ship, the *Antarctic* over 60 deaths were reported from smallpox on a single voyage.

It wasn't until 1840 that the Atlantic crossing became reasonably tolerable in steerage because of the greater size of the new steamships. A great improvement came with Robert Napier's design of a sharp cut water bow that allowed easier passage of the steamship through heavy seas and greatly increased its speed.

In 1843 the *Great Britain* became the first passenger vessel made of iron to cross the Atlantic by use of the screw propeller. The journey was not only faster, but much more comfortable (the *Great Western*, though it had utilized the screw propeller, was not manufactured of iron). One of the most important developments in the history of seafaring, the unique propulsion device had been introduced by Francis Pettit Smith in 1836. Brunel was one of the first to realize its advantages over the paddle wheel. The British Government was also quick to take notice.

In 1845, in order to determine the efficiency of the screw propeller for its warships, the British Admiralty staged a tug-of-war between *HMS Rattler*, with a screw propeller designed by Brunel, and the *Alecto*, powered by paddle wheels. Both ships were of the same tonnage with equal power, but the *Rattler* towed away its rival at a steady speed. The Admiralty was convinced: the paddle wheel was doomed (though not used on ocean voyages, it remained perfectly suitable for rivers and inland waterways).

Despite these improvements in ocean travel, as late as 1849, ten years after the Thomas family had sailed on the *Roscius*, advice was given in a London Magazine for people not to venture the Atlantic journey if they were afraid. If circumstances were such that they had to make the voyage, then they should take some tea and other comforts to help out the meager rations on board ship.

For seasickness, there was no effective cure, although the newspapers were full of supposed cures sent in by people who had made the crossing. Many of these, such as "try to drink lots of sea-water," were positively harmful. Despite the well-founded fears of the Atlantic crossing, however, adverse conditions in Wales (and especially in Ireland) kept the emigrant ships fully occupied.

The success of the Atlantic packets led to Cunard entering the race for the Atlantic trade and the competition for emigrant fares with the Britannia, its first liner. This iron-built, steam-powered vessel crossed the Atlantic from Halifax to Bristol in fourteen and a half days. The Collins Line of New York was quickly organized to compete directly with Cunard for the Atlantic trade.

Fourteen years after his arrival in New York, David was saddened to learn that, after many years of gallant service crossing the Atlantic, the *Roscius* was severely damaged in a violent storm in January, 1853 when four of her crew were washed overboard. The magnificent ship finally sank in the North Atlantic in 1860. On January 10, 1841, the gallant little *Mountaineer* had been lost when it struck the rocks in the Menai Straits in North Wales and sank with no hope of recovery. In the meantime, David had rapidly been fulfilling all the expectations of the Lehigh Company.

Chapter Seven

Conditions in Wales: Unemployment, Drink and Temperance.

During the middle years of the 19th century, poor conditions in Wales in both agriculture and industry hastened the flow of emigrants to the United States and other countries. News of David Thomas's success provided an impetus for many more Welshmen to follow him to America. A letter he was sent on December 29, 1841 shows an attitude typical of many workmen back home at the time. The body of the letter is written entirely in Welsh by John Prytherch, who signs off, however, in English as "your humble servant."

Prytherch wrote from Defynog where, he says, the Thomas family was very much missed. The loss was keenly felt in church, particularly, and by David's former companions and work mates. A great deal of the temperance movement had died out in the area, he lamented, but the writer was pleased toadd that there was still something of it left.

The letter goes on to describe the terrible weather, with incessant rain, but then the clouds had lifted and the floods had finally cleared. Unfortunately, the year's supply of hay had been ruined, and there had been additional great losses right through the winter up until the present time. Money was scarce, and there was little work.

John's letter continued the litany of woes: it appeared to be getting worse every day, and hundreds were out of work, not just in South Wales, but in all parts of Britain. Many were leaving the country to go to Australia and to New Zealand, with the iron industry supporting the poor in their passage. Hundreds were also going to America, including whole families, while thousands remained who didn't know what to do.

John explained that his own son was going to America along with many others, so he and his wife had decided to emigrate as well. They want to know if Thomas can give them some advice what he should do and to tell him about the country where he is now living. If David can see that it would be better for the Prytherch family to come over to Pennsylvania, would David answer right away? The description of the terrible conditions in Wales is continued in the next letter, from one of David's cousins.

This letter was sent from Victoria Iron Works, Monmouthshire. It is addressed simply to "David Thomas at Allentown, Pennsylvania." Written by William John, who calls himself a "Bridge Stocker" (stoker), it is typical of so many letters written by those who were being forced to emigrate from their homeland by poor economic conditions in the whole of Britain, but in South Wales in particular.

William's first language is Welsh as his English is full of misspellings and grammatical errors. No doubt impressed with the early accomplishments of David Thomas, he also states that he is desirous of seeing America. He had never determined to put that desire into execution until now, he says, "the state of our country being so bad and the price of oppression and poverty being so great everywhere," and he himself "a sufferer in these distressing times as well as my neighbours and countrymen."

William has decided to leave his native land and wants David to find employment for himself and his family in Pennsylvania. He also requests the loan of a few pounds to defray part of their expenses which he will leave in David's hands how he can afford to repay. His family consists of his wife and five children, four girls and one boy — "all of them fine, healthy children." He is not out of employment, but wages are very low and "every eating article is very dear".

William continues by stating that while God blesses him with health and strength, he is determined to try to do better for his family, and he is anxious to try his fortune in another country. He will part with his native land without regret and leave it in the hands of those "who have no heart to quit it." He wants to know the wages of the ironworkers where David works and needs directions how to travel to Pennsylvania and where the nearest port is located.

William also wants to know if the family should bring their feather beds with them. He tells David that he is a good worker, and that he can undertake either the mine burning or lime burning or work as a founder or filler or as "Occation Ingihnere" (occasion engineer?). The letter continues: "Lewis Caarfilly, blocklayer, also wishes to be remembered and would accompany the family to America if David promises them employment."

We do not know Thomas's answer to this and to many other similar letters. We also do not know how many of his former friends and work mates followed him to America. From the rapid development of the Welsh settlement at Catasauqua, centered around the iron works, and the presence of a Welsh chapel and Sunday school, which David established there before the end of 1840, it must have been a considerable number. The expansion of the iron and coal industries in Pennsylvania during the middle years of the century certainly made that state a magnet for most of the Welsh immigrants to the United States. Opportunities in the anthracite regions seemed too promising to be ignored.

On September 30, 1839, Mr. John Walters used the English language to begin another letter to David Thomas containing more news of the dreadful weather in Wales, with incessant rain and the ruin of the hay crops after what had been an extremely hot fortnight. Then follows some news of family and friends and various happenings at the Brecon Forest Company before the writer switches to the Welsh language to describe the great work being done by the Dirwest, the temperance society, with "upwards of two or three hundred members in good spirits having met at Castellnedd" (Neath).

"Thanks to the great king of heaven and earth," continues Walters, "they [members of the temperance movement] have managed to break the teeth of the opposition, even though many have been trying to strangle their movement under the guise of abstainers." We remember, of course, that the Thomas family was committed to total abstinence from all alcohol. As superintendent at Ynyscedwyn, he had seen the effects of drink upon his workmen and upon the industry in which they were employed.

During the 1830's and 1840's, editorials in *The Cambrian* roundly denounced drinking as one of the causes of the great civil unrest taking place all over Britain. The leaders of the Chartists were severely castigated in the newspapers for their supposed drinking habits. What was overlooked, however, was that merely drinking water in the country was perhaps the most dangerous habit of all.

Even in the nation's capital, London, fresh, clean water was hard to find. Cholera and other diseases were epidemic. Michael Faraday, the distinguished chemist observed that the River Thames, as it ran by the Houses of Parliament, was "a fermenting sewer" in which "near the bridges, the feculence rolled up in clouds so dense that they were visible at the surface."

In Merthyr Tydfil, rapidly becoming the largest town in Wales at that time, there were only three water pumps to serve a population of over 40,000, and the water was all too often contaminated. Outbreaks of cholera were all too frequent in the area. Cemeteries were running out of room in which to bury the dead. Milk, produced in most unsanitary conditions and never pasteurized, was still very dangerous to drink, though the connection with tuberculosis had not been firmly established; and tea was still a very expensive rarity.

On the other hand, beer was plentiful, could be produced locally, and it was cheap. Throughout the century, Wales was predominantly a beer-drinking country, especially when prices were further reduced by a repeal of the duty through the Beer Act of 1830. The main diet of the majority of the working population seems to have been buttermilk, potatoes, and oatmeal, with small quantities of salted meat and fish added when available. All was quaffed down by prodigious quantities of beer, which was believed to impart physical strength and stamina.

When bread and tea became cheaper and more readily available, the converts to "tea-totalism" were pleasantly surprised to find that abstention from beer did not at all weaken them. Consumption of beer, however, remained high. Beer was used to kill pain, and beer drinking was closely connected to the various festivals and days of the calendar; it also helped commemorate the chief turning points of the "rites of passage" in one's life. But public drunkenness was common throughout the country.

Intoxication and fighting were widespread; not a day passed in Wales without lurid accounts being reported in the newspapers of horrible deaths, mutilations, with fights and robberies all too common, not to mention the accidental deaths such as drowning, etc., caused by drinking. It is of interest to note that whenever someone was fished out of a river or a canal or the docks as a result of being drowned while intoxicated - an event reported almost daily - the only remedy used by physicians to try to restore life to the poor soul was that of bloodletting. Needless to say, their attempts were none too successful.

Despite the growth of the temperance movement in the middle part of the century, the use of beer continued to play its customary prominent part of the social life of Wales. In West Wales for example, there was a custom in which announcements were issued to solicit gifts at a bidding, held before a marriage, accompanied by a "bid-ale" or "cwrw bach" (small beer feast) when beer was sold to raise money for the wedding couple.

There were also "cwrw gwadd," beer feasts held when someone was ill or who had been in an accident in which money was charged and given to the family. At funeral processions, home-made beer was provided for the mourners, and it also accompanied sales and auctions, each bidder being given a glass of beer. Some vicars were reported as giving tickets to their parishioners, entitling them to so much beer when their tithes were collected. And we mustn't forget the shameful custom of bribes of free beer at election time.

Theaters in Wales were for all intents and purposes non-existent; what little dramatic productions there were consisted mainly of traveling interludes, put on wherever a suitable space could be found. The public houses, on the other hand, were the centers of literary and cultural activity in many parts of the country, serving as headquarters of various societies. With the lack of suitable indoor meeting places, many reformists, including the Chartists, also held their lodge meetings in taverns, which thus took a large share of the blame for the civil disturbances and great riots of the 1830's.

A reaction to all this drinking was furthered by the newspapers, by the Church, and of course by the temperance societies, who published as many as fourteen journals in the Welsh language alone by 1850. The temperance reformers held the view that the drinking place was a hotbed of vice where "crimes were planned, stolen goods received, drunkenness created, and prostitution carried on." They may have been partly correct.

The Beer Act of 1830 had been passed as the free traders' remedy for the drink problem. The intention was to make beer accessible and cheap so that supply would settle down to meet demand and the level of drunkenness fall off. It was also passed because of impending fears of another disastrous "gin age" from which the whole country had suffered so severely during the waning years of the previous century. But when prices of spirits were raised and prices of beer lowered, the opposite effect took place: beer houses quickly proliferated, and drunkenness increased.

In Dowlais alone, a district of Merthyr, in the early part of the nineteenth century there were more than 200 taverns. Incredible as it seems in retrospect, as many as one in every three eligible voters in a list of 643 in Merthyr and Dowlais was a publican or keeper of a beer-house.

It is important to remember, however, when dealing with the problem of drinking, that when cholera struck, as it did so often in the crowded towns of the industrial districts, beer was drunk as an anesthetic. At the time, to be fair to the people of Wales, excessive beer drinking was not just their problem alone. Ten-year old schoolboys at Eton and Harrow, England's most exclusive schools, were given copious quantities of beer to drink at breakfast and possibly more at supper. In the 1840's, in South Wales, with massive immigration from Ireland, the problem got worse again. In industry there was at least one whole day a week lost to absenteeism due to drink.

Local forces of law and order were totally inadequate to take care of any trouble in the streets caused by excessive drinking. In Bridgend, near Cardiff, for example, according to *The Cambrian*, the whole police force of that town consisted of a shoemaker over 60 years old and a young tailor, "both of whom were often found in a state of complete intoxication."

It is no wonder that the temperance movement grew rapidly in an attempt to put things right. The euphoria in Walters' letter to David Thomas in Allentown over the rise of the temperance movement in Wales is somewhat ironic, however, for the movement had begun in the United States in the mid-twenties. Following this lead, the British and Foreign Temperance Society was founded in London in 1831. The movement reached Wales only after successful progress through Ireland, Scotland and Northern England.

The first Welsh temperance societies were established among the large Welsh populations of Liverpool and Manchester, in northern England, where they often flourished as 'friendly societies," taking the place of the community ties that had given structure to their lives in rural Wales. In 1832, a society was formed in Wales proper, in Clwyd in the Northeast.

At first, some of these societies, were in effect, moderation societies, allowing up to two pints of beer a day per drinker, except on Sundays, but by 1835 the movement was devoted to total abstinence, termed tea-totalism. It was to such a society in Ystradgynlais that David Thomas and George Crane belonged.

In 1836 *The Dirwestydd* ("the teetotaler") first appeared, with over 4,000 copies a month printed by 1838. Also in 1836 the first temperance society was established in South Wales when the preacher and lecturer David Rees of Llanelli came to Cardiff. By 1838, tea-totalism had completely usurped moderation as the most popular solution to the drink problem in the British

Isles. In Wales, the leading advocate of temperance was the Reverend Evan Davies who wrote a series of articles in *Y Dysgedydd* ('the teacher") based on American or Irish temperance tracts, especially those of Father Walker in Ireland, who was winning thousands of converts.

If today, Wales is known internationally as "The Land of Song," it was the temperance movement that first gave impetus to choral singing in South Wales. Choral Societies were founded as one solution to the drink problem to help people through the worst consequences of industrialization by occupying their time and by keeping them away from the taverns. On Christmas Day, 1837 a temperance procession marched in Dowlais, joined by choirs from neighboring towns.

Following the success of that first choral event, it was not too long before an annual festival of choirs was initiated by the Gwent and Glamorgan Temperance Movement. At the Eisteddfod at Aberdare in 1846 (perhaps the first truly "National" eisteddfod of Wales), choral competition was added to the list of events. It has remained one of the most popular and well-attended of all the competitions ever since.

By the early 1860's the tradition of the Cymanfa Ganu (a chapel meeting held expressly for the singing of hymns) had become firmly established as a major Welsh cultural tradition. It was helped greatly by the publication in 1859 of *Llyfr Tonnau Cynulleidfaol* ("the Congregational Tune Book") edited by one of Wales's best hymn-tune writers with the bardic name of Ieuan Gwyllt. This became one of the most popular books ever published in Wales.

Not all in Wales favored choral singing and temperance, however. There was some opposition to the temperance movement from farmers in particular, because they grew the barley that was a prime ingredient of beer. And the many publicans were also opposed to the new movement. Despite its rapid growth and its thousands of converts, by the early 1840's, thanks to such opposition, the temperance movement was practically a spent force. Its initial euphoria and its early enthusiasm had quickly waned according to one writer, when feelings of the expected millenium declined, and when economic hardships made many of its early advocates turn back to drink in an attempt to ease their troubles.

But troubles continued. A letter from John Walters sent in January, 1840, contains more diatribes against the Brecon Forest Company, a mention of the cost of imported American flour at 58 pence a sack, and a question to Thomas about the state of religion in the neighborhood of Allentown. "Do you know anything," asks Walters, "of the Reverend Moses Parry's mission to America?"

Walters had seen a letter from Moses Parry from Stuben (sic) that had a great effect on his mind. Despite all the troubles in Wales, people there were highly concerned over the fate of their fellow-Welshmen in America, some of whom had settled in an area around Steuben, New York State.

The question about the Moses Parry mission refers to the sailing of the Reverend Henry Rees of Liverpool and the Reverend Moses Parry of Denbigh on the Liverpool early in May of that year. They had been sent as a deputation from the associated body of Welsh Calvinistic Methodists to visit their countrymen, "who reside in great numbers in various parts of the United States." Walters' letter concludes with his pleasure at Mrs. Thomas's going to school in America to learn English.

In his lengthy letter of January 28, Mr. Walters provides Thomas news about the Dirwest Society meetings and a very successful revival at Cwmgoed, "with the works at rest and everywhere crammed with people from 10 o'clock in the morning until 9 at night. "They are hoping," he continues, "to hear many again asking the way to grow with their faces hitherwards." He writes glowingly of Dirwest, which was "everywhere preparing the way of the Lord in the preaching of the Gospel of our salvation." A day had been appointed in Britain and America that month for fasting ñ "a project that was being kept with great solemnity in most of the churches in Wales."

Walters goes on to tell Thomas that it would be important to establish a Welsh cause in his vicinity (Catasauqua, Pennsylvania). He then asks him to try to locate the son of an uncle of his from Merthyr who had been in America for many years but who had not been heard of for the last three. The man is described as a marble mason, a very clever fellow.' "It was he who built the furnaces in America for Mr. Thomas who is now at "Stratyfora." (Walter may have been confused with the place name: Thomas had employed the marble mason at Catasauqua; Walters is confused as to place names). Walters continues, "I wish you could find him or hear something of him whether dead or alive."

Later that year, another letter from John Walters refers to a communication from Henry Rees, who had written about "the deplorable state of the Welch (sic) in America for want of means of Grace." Rees's letter had created a sensation in Welsh religious circles, and the matter was being given serious consideration in both North and South Wales. In both areas, wrote Walters, "they intend doing something about it in the next spring to send preachers over."

Mr. Rees had recommended that two or three ministers be sent over with their salaries paid so that they would remain respectable and be able to devote all their time to work of the ministry. Other ministers could be sent over who, after settling themselves in America, would be able to maintain themselves through some secular employment and make themselves useful by preaching occasionally in the different countries."

It is apparent that religion was still being taken very seriously in the Wales of the 19th century. In what can today be considered a touch of real irony, *The Cambrian* enthusiastically reported in December, 1840 that a theatre in Oldham, England had just been converted into a chapel by the Wesleyan Methodists. Just over one hundred and fifty years later, Welsh newspapers would contain many instances of the reverse happening, with chapels being converted into theatres, bowling alleys, Bingo halls, or other places of entertainment.

Walters' letter continues to state that the weather was "very serious for the harvest," and there had not been two consecutive fine days for the past nine weeks. Regarding the weather in Britain that year, *The Cambrian* reported that there had been very favorable conditions for planting earlier with hardly any frost and very mild weather in February. But there had been a heavy snowfall during the running of the races at Epsom Downs on Derby Day (May 22) where, in addition to snow, there had been a freezing northeast wind. In South Wales, there had also been a heavy snowstorm during the hay harvest in the same month.

The letter then contains a note written by John's wife, Mary Walters, who says she shall be inclined to come over but circumstances will not admit it yet, "though they look better than when you left." She also asks Thomas to let them know if it were any advantage to take feather beds over to America, and earthenware. John then concludes the letter by writing of the most deplorable weather they have been having "for so long a time," and asks for blessings for his friend overseas.

On October 1, 1839, Mr. Llewellyn Jeffreys wrote to David Thomas. Jeffreys had been one of the engineers at the Brecon Forest Company when David Thomas was in their employ. It is written from Castell du Wharf, Brecon, in what is obviously a well-educated hand, though rather pompous in tone. We remember that during slack times at Ynyscedwyn, David had moved with his family to Castell Ddu Wharf, the northern terminus of the Brecon Forest Tramroad.

In order to increase the scope of his business, but also in order to better educate his children, David had sold domestic and agricultural hardware as well as coal and lime in addition to working as a manager on the tramway. It was at Castell Ddu that he had first been introduced to Erskine Hazard by George Crane.

Much of Jeffreys' letter is an apology for not writing sooner, with the addition of some family news. According to the writer, the Sunday school is well attended, but the temperance people, while very much alive, were not as numerous as they had when Thomas left for America.

Mr. Jeffreys next gives the information that a Mr. James Smith was desirous of going over to America in the next spring, and the writer himself would visit David Thomas, if the latter would tell him the best time to travel, for he wished to obtain a situation there. (Subsequent letters reveal that Jeffreys did not go to America after all). David Jones the millwright also wanted to emigrate and wished to know if there was any place in America that wanted him.

At this stage in the exchange of letters, it is a bit of a puzzle why Mr Jeffreys expresses a wish to emigrate. Despite some earlier problems with the construction of the Tramway, he had just become one of the directors of the

Brecon Forest Company. Since Crane's use of the hot blast to smelt iron with anthracite, prospects for all classes of industry in South West Wales, at least on the surface, appeared highly promising.

In March of that year (1839), the Ynyscedwyn Iron works had been advertising for three good finers "to whom constant work and liberal wages will be given." In May the same company advertised for two "keepers of Founders" for one of the blast furnaces. The request was for "steady, sober men who understand their business [who] will meet with constant employment and good wages."

Perhaps David Thomas's success in Pennsylvania may have tempted Jeffreys, who seemed to be having some problems with his company, despite his high position. Also tempting must have been the long lists of daily notices in the newspapers for the "fine new American ships" sailing regularly to the United States and Canada.

Perhaps the main reason for Jeffreys' wish to emigrate at this time, however, can be found in the social upheavals taking place in Britain, with strong repercussions being felt in the South Wales coal fields. The "dreadful business" of the Chartists referred to by Mr. Walters in his letter was beginning to make its mark in the area. Its progress was being closely followed in the pages of that most conservative of British newspapers, *The Cambrian*.

Chapter Eight

The Effects of the Chartist Movement on Wales

Not long after David had arrived in Allentown, a much-relieved George Crane had written to him that the spirit of Chartism had not yet taken root in the Ystradgynlais district, but mention of the Chartists reaching the area appears when Mr. Walters describes them in his letter to David Thomas as "going on at a dreadful rate."

Both writers were referring to the new popular movement named after a London radical Williams Levett, who drafted a bill known as The People's Charter in May, 1838. "I do not know," Crane wrote in September, 1839, "where this dreadful business will end." Little did he know, in his isolated position as owner of the iron works, set apart from his workers, that "a dreadful business" was just about to begin.

Levett had been inspired by the work of Henry Hunt, nicknamed "Orator" by adoring crowds, who came to listen to his speeches denouncing his fellow landowners and advocating a repeal of the notorious Corn Laws. In the North of England in 1819, at St. Peter's Fields, Manchester, a crowd estimated at 80,000 gathered to hear Hunt expound his ideas on the need for annual parliaments and for a greatly enlarged electorate. When a troop of cavalry with drawn sabers tried to arrest the speaker, the crowd panicked.

In the ensuing melee, eleven people were killed, either by the bayonet, or by being trampled on by the horses. For his part, Hunt was sentenced to two and a half years imprisonment. The whole affair was named "the Peterloo Massacre." It had the effect of quelling any such disturbances for the time being.

Just to make sure, the government passed *The Six Acts* in December. Public meetings were severely curtailed; training in the use of firearms was forbidden; magistrates were empowered to search for and to confiscate arms; provisions were made for speedy trials in "cases of misdemeanor"; penalties were increased for seditious libel; and radical journalism was effectively limited by the imposition of the newspaper stamp duty on all periodicals containing news.

Apart from a few isolated incidents, there seems to have been comparatively little unrest in South Wales especially among the rural population of

Glamorganshire. For one thing, wages were much higher there mainly because the farmers had to compete with the rapidly developing coal, metallurgical and transport industries, which were attracting laborers in great numbers from all parts of Wales, but especially the farming areas of the southwest.

In the Swansea Valley, in towns such as Ystradgynlais, where the Ynyscedwyn Iron Works was situated, many newcomers had come from the counties of Carmarthenshire, Breconshire, and Pembrokeshire looking for work. They were not too much concerned over political matters. Thus they were not too interested in the philosophies of Chartism; they were more concerned with the difficult task of finding employment and making a living.

But there had been unrest in the mining districts situated farther east, in the Valleys, areas of heavy immigration from other parts of Britain and especially from Ireland, with its long history of resistance to various and all kinds of authority.

The great depression of 1829 had led to massive unemployment and wage cuts in the industrial districts of southeast Wales. Among the working population of Merthyr in particular, there were substantial debts. This situation, in turn had led to a credit crisis among the shopkeepers and tradesmen, with the Court of Requests (the Debtor's Court) engaged in widespread confiscation of property.

Demanding redress of their grievances, in a demonstration led by Thomas Llewelyn, a Cyfartha miner, a large crowd set free the prisoners in the local gaol. Llewelyn then led a march to the neighboring town of Aberdare where one of the crowd's demands was the equalization of wages.

At the same time, at Hirwain, a few miles distant, when the Court seized a truck belonging to Lewis Lewis, alarmed miners and iron puddlers joined with political radicals and raised the red flag of rebellion — the first time it was to be so used in Britain. On its staff was impaled a loaf of bread, symbol of the needs of the crowd. It had a magical effect.

The ever-growing crowd, probably emboldened by copious supplies of cheap beer, marched on Merthyr, raiding shops and houses and seizing property and goods earlier confiscated by the Court and restored them to their former owners. In defiance of the British Government's Riot Act, they drove off the magistrates and special constables that had been hurriedly assembled to stop them and burned the Court itself. A troop of Scottish Highlanders was then sent from Brecon Barracks to restore order. When the crowd marched to the doors of the Castle Inn, the soldiers waiting inside opened fire.

In the ensuing confusion, over two dozen workers were killed and hundreds wounded. But the soldiers lost 16 men and were forced into retreat. The crowd, described in *The Cambrian* as "thousands of men and women and a body of Irishmen carrying clubs" then set up camp outside town near Cefn Coed, where they ambushed and disarmed fresh military reinforcements sent from barracks in England.

Other ambushes prevented the military from crushing the workers. In the long run, however, the rebels failed; their numbers were too few, their arms too pitiful, and their supporters too weak and afraid of severe repercussions from the armed might of the British government. A planned attack on Cyfarthfa Castle, home of the Crawshays, came to nought. Fearful of losing more men to well-directed volleys from the military, the uprising soon petered out in confusion and lack of direction.

An entry in *Mrs. Arbuthnot's Diary* of June, 1831 expresses the general feeling in England towards the events in South Wales. She writes: "There has been a great riot in Wales and the soldiers have killed twenty-four people. When two or three were killed at Manchester, it was called the Peterloo Massacre, and the newspapers for weeks wrote it up as the most outrageous and wicked proceeding ever heard of. But that was in Tory times; now this Welsh riot is scarcely mentioned."

The seeds of rebellion had been sown in the South Wales Valleys. Though the Merthyr Rising had started as a purely local rebellion against unjust conditions in the mines and iron works, it had quickly developed into an armed insurrection. Similar grievances over low wages, poor municipal administration and the desperate need for parliamentary reform was sparking such local risings all over Britain.

In Parliament, Lord Melbourne, who had advocated severe repression of all popular workers' movements, declared that South Wales was now "the worst and most formidable district in the kingdom." He was determined to use every possible means to crush "unlawful assemblages of armed individuals." Thus, despite many initial successes on local levels, the movement could not possibly succeed.

Faced by massive military strength, the determination of the British Government to restore public order at all costs, and the antagonism of the majority of the loyal inhabitants of South Wales, the workers' movement soon collapsed. At the Cardiff assizes in June of that year, retribution for the revolt led to the trial of 28 scapegoats, mostly ironstone miners and puddlers, but including two women.

Lewis Lewis was sentenced to death, but his sentence was commuted to life imprisonment in Van Diemen's Land (Australia). Richard Lewis, known as Dic Penderyn, was not so fortunate; he was hanged for the crime of shooting and wounding a soldier, though he vigorously protested his innocence and there were no sworn witnesses to the alleged assault.

It is recorded that the last words Lewis spoke on the scaffold were "O Arglwydd, dyma gamwedd (Oh Lord, what an injustice) — words that were to make the poor man a martyr to the people of the Valleys. (Forty years later, Ieuan Parker, of Cwmafan, who had emigrated to the United States, confessed to the crime for which Lewis had been hanged).

As serious as the riots had been, the deaths incurred at the hands of the military, and the hanging of Richard Lewis attracted little attention in the English newspapers. The event at Manchester took precedence in the public imagination over the much more serious business that happened in South Wales. In the English press, as usual, there was general indifference to the plight of the Welsh workers and their families.

The collapse of the workers' movement at Merthyr did not end their grievances. It was not difficult to find reasons for the "troubles" that now begun seriously to affect all the South Wales mining valleys. In the early 1830's in Glamorgan, the discovery of coal had brought rapid and massive immigration into the new industrial settlements. Merthyr and Aberdare had been the fastest growing communities and also the centers of the most serious disturbances. They were simply following a radical tradition begun half a century before.

As early as 1793, several hundred copper workers and colliers had marched on Swansea demanding a reduction in the prices of grain, cheese, and butter and seeking higher wages. In 1801 three Merthyr men had been sentenced to death for rioting. They had merely been protesting the high price of bread.

The Corn Laws, passed in Parliament in 1815, and vigorously retained, meant that the price of bread was kept artificially high to benefit the landed interests and wealthy farmers. By 1839 a collier or ironworker with a wife and four children needed three bushels of wheat a month that cost 45 shillings. At the time average wages were about 18 shillings a week or 72 shillings a month. But when unions were formed to try to bring about better conditions, they were met with harshly.

In the 1820's, at David Thomas's old place of employment, the Neath Abbey Works, fifty men were fired immediately after they had tried to form a union, and the rest of the workers, fearful for their jobs, voted to abandon the idea. The local press, in particular *The Cambrian*, published scathing attacks on the unions and their members, portraying their leaders as "gin-swilling degenerates."

In 1831, the influential Calvinistic Methodists also publicly condemned trade unionism and called on all Church members who had joined a union to leave it immediately. The times were not yet ripe for the coming of unionism. The Chartists seemed to offer a better way. They naively believed that they could somehow bring about a democratic Parliament and an enfranchised working class that would be able to redress their grievances. Alas, as it turned out, they were far too premature in their hopes.

There were other causes of social unrest that manifested themselves in Wales, especially in the agricultural Southwest, where the most tangible and visible symbols of the discontent were the numerous toll-gates on the turnpike roads and their excessive rates. Towns such as Carmarthen were surrounded by such toll-gates, and farmers especially were hard-hit by the excessive tolls on such necessities as lime and the transportation of livestock.

One night in May, 1839, at Efailwen, just outside Carmarthen, the toll gates were destroyed when a group of about 400 people dressed as women drove away the special constables gathered to protect the gates. The leader of the protestors, reputed to be Thomas Rees, known as Twm Carnabwth, was disguised in the clothes of a local woman named Rebecca.

Disturbances continued for a number of years, with large crowds burning and destroying tollgates and work-houses. It wasn't until a government commission had recommended reduction of tolls, especially on lime and other agricultural products, that the *Rebecca Riots*, as they were known, came to an end.

The rise throughout the whole of Britain of Chartism, the popular movement that George Crane had so greatly feared, constituted a much more serious threat to the public order. On March 16, 1839, it was reported in *The Cambrian* that in the House of Lords, the Duke of Buckingham inquired whether the Government had become acquainted with the fact that certain persons, calling themselves Chartists, had provided themselves with arms. Lord Melbourne's reply was that he was perfectly well aware of the report to that effect. The House took immediate action.

On May 11, it was reported that the Queen issued a proclamation for the suppression of meetings for the purpose of military training and also for the suppression of unlawful assemblages of armed individuals. The proclamation stated that such meetings had been going on in the United Kingdom, and instructions were given for them to be put down, suppressed, and the offenders brought to justice. The government greatly feared that the Chartists would lead a general insurrection throughout the land.

The government's fears may have been partly justified. Chartism was growing into a mass movement in favor of social and political reform, gathering impressive, massive strength during the economic depression of the 1830's. It soon swelled to national importance under the vigorous leadership of the Irishman Feargus Edward O'Connor. In the industrial valleys of South Wales the movement received a warm welcome, attracting a large following among the largely immigrant miners and iron workers, many of them also Irish.

The Cambrian of May 11, 1839 noted that a large number of colliers in the hills of Tredegar had given notice to discontinue work, and the leaders of the Chartists were to give a demonstration so that a large number of those who were out of employment would join them. A meeting was to take place at Duke's Town, about a mile beyond Tredegar.

According to *The Cambrian*, showing itself as ever a most pro-government and anti-Chartist publication, considerable apprehension was felt by the peaceable inhabitants of Tredegar, and Mr. Samuel Homfray, acting magistrate for the district, with other magistrates, took efforts to preserve the public peace. No beer was to be sold at any public houses or beer shops from 12 o'clock until six the following morning. Precautions were taken and, according to the paper, the inhabitants of Tredegar waited with "anxious curiosity."

It appeared that a serious riot was about to take place, but the arrival of the authorities, including the military, led to a rapid dispersal of the crowd. The whole event was labelled a complete failure by the editors of *The Cambrian*, who condescendingly wrote: "The town assumed its wonted aspect after the departure of the Chartists, and it is generally believed, the ill success of this essay will deter them from exhibiting their wickedness and folly in that neighborhood again."

The same paper contained another article entitled "Chartist Outrage," giving an account of what it termed a "serious riot " at Llanidloes (a town in mid-Wales. This article was interposed with one of a meeting at Risca where Edwards the Baker, who had led the procession at Tredegar, spoke of that meeting as having been extremely successful, with 3,000 present.

The account stated that Edwards had made "a disgusting exhibition of himself" and had been openly repudiated by Jones and others, who had played an active part with him. They consequently had cut their connection with one whose conduct was termed by the paper as "disgraceful, even to Chartism."

Having been first apprehended for rioting, the Chartists were stated by the paper as having come armed with guns, pistols, pikes, and bludgeons to the Trewythen Arms, where they broke doors and windows to force their way in; rescued the parties that had been apprehended previously; nearly killed the police officers; turned the landlord and his family out of the house, and completely ransacked the whole place.

According to *The Cambrian*, the rioters even went so far as to "run a pike through the hat of the resident magistrate." In the face of this so-called threat to the British Crown, the Montgomeryshire Militia were ordered to hold themselves ready to act, and if necessary, the South Salopian Yeomanry "will be instantly marched to the neighborhood." Much the same apprehension was felt farther south, in the vicinity of Newport.

Chapter Nine

The Newport Rising.

The May 11, 1839 edition of *The Cambrian* had a lengthy and very apprehensive report of the arrival of the Military at Newport, site of a forthcoming major Chartist rally. The Lord Lieutenant of Monmouthshire had sent a division of "the gallant 29th," consisting of a field officer, a distinguished officer, Major Wrotterslay, two captains, four subalterns, a surgeon, seven sergeants, and one hundred and five rank and file." The troops arrived on a packet ship from Bristol and according to the paper, "were welcomed by the people."

The edition also reported an anti-Chartist meeting at Coalbrook Vale in the Merthyr district, during the previous April composed of "the oldest and most respected residents"—chaired by Crawshay Bailey (the iron Master of Dowlais, who had fortified his mansion against possible assault by the workers). Bailey's statements, the iron master claimed, were made "to counteract the baneful effects of the principles of the Chartists and to show the inhabitants of this place who are their real friends" (himself and the Iron masters, of course). He had known some of them (the protesting workers) for twenty years or more, he said, and they should be grateful for his favors as "none of the Chartists will give them employment."

In his speech, Bailey bragged that "fifty years ago, in this valley, nothing could be heard from Brynmawr to Aberbeeg but the sound of a single blacksmith's hammer — and there were only 200 inhabitants; but now there may be heard the sound of machinery employed in converting the minerals that then lay buried under these mountains into finished iron, and there were more than 10,000 people in the district." He would, he continued, "sacrifice his life, rather than lose any of his property."

Condemning the demands of the Chartists, the iron master stated that "annual parliaments would be a great evil, as members of the working class would think of nothing but continual electioneering." Before ending his speech, Bailey added that any complaints against taxation were erroneous "as such monies return to you like the tides flow up the rivers."

Other speeches in similar vein then followed by many distinguished gentlemen of the area, some in Welsh, some in English, but all speaking out against the evils of Chartism, the goodness of the British Constitution, and the need for loyalty to it and to the Crown. All the speakers took pains to contrast "the happy, well-fed, well-housed working classes of Britain" with those who lived in other countries such as Canada and France, "where revolution or Roman Catholicism or laziness and dishonesty had caused butchery and inhumanity so much in contrast to Britain."

The crowd was told that they should not let themselves be goaded into insubordination and disaffection through men like Vincent and Stephens, the prominent Chartist leaders, who would bring calamity to all "through their appeals for such abominations as *universal suffrage* (italics mine). The very term brought shivers to the landed, privileged classes who alone had the power to vote and who controlled every aspect of the workers' lives.

But many poor working people had little reason to believe such rhetoric, especially from the iron-masters who exploited their labor. Not seeing themselves as happy, well-fed, and well-housed at all, they preferred to trust and to follow men like Vincent and Stephens. There were also thousands of unemployed in the five great Welsh Valleys. Mr. Bailey, of course, neglected that his own family had chosen to live in a fortified round house, specially constructed at Nantyglo for their own protection in case of a workers' uprising.

Serious riots at Nantyglo had broken out in 1816 and again in 1822. They were suppressed by companies of Scots Greys brought in whenever trouble loomed. But these were local disturbances. A more general crisis occurred early in 1839 when the Great Chartist Convention met in London, with the people of Wales represented by Hugh Williams, Charles Jones and John Frost. The Petition drawn up at the Convention contained more than one and a quarter-million signatures. Originating in Birmingham, in the Midlands, it had been adopted and signed in towns all over Britain.

The Cambrian, in one of its more-enlightened editorials, described the men who signed as "honest, sober, and industrious." They merely wanted the House to be anxious to relieve "the sufferings and redress the wrongs of the working classes, which they believed to be their right, as enjoying the privileges of British subjects." If the House would not give them that — "a fair day's pay for a fair day's work and good food and clothing for their families," then they would put forward every means which the law allowed to change the representation of the House.

The House of Commons at the time was discussing the abolition of slavery in the British Empire and the imposition of some sort of national education system in Britain. Under these circumstances, conditions would certainly have seemed favorable for the presentation of the Petition, which was presented on June 14.

The six points of the Charter were universal male suffrage, vote by ballot, equal electoral districts, annual parliaments, abolition of the property qualification for election to Parliament, and payment for Members (so that the election could be open to all classes).

Dominated by mercantile and manufacturing interests, the Government took little notice of the Petition. In a gesture so very typical of the attitude of so many of its members, not only did the House refuse to listen to the requests of the Chartists, but it went ahead to prepare measures to suppress the movement, ruthlessly if necessary.

In response, in Wales, as in many parts of England, throughout the year, huge, open-air protest meetings were held. In many of these, representatives of the "Physical Force Group," as opposed to the "Moral Force" groups thought it necessary to arm themselves in whatever manner was possible. In May, Henry Vincent, who was one of the movement's most brilliant orators, was arrested as a threat to the peace, and others were arrested soon afterwards. Several clashes with the authorities then took place.

When the Convention in London was unable to act effectively and its appeals overwhelmingly rejected by Parliament, it dissolved itself. More determined and forceful men then took over the leadership. In South Wales, such activists as John Frost, Zephania Williams, and John Rees pressed for revolutionary policy.

At the same time, at Bath, in England, a meeting was described in which over 2000 Chartists took part, of whom a great proportion were women. "After several inflammatory harangues", stated *The Cambrian*, the meeting dispersed and the utterly discomforted Chartists returned "quite chop-fallen" to their homes (in reality, they were probably jubilant at having such a large turnout).

Other Chartists were reported as being arrested at Birmingham "in opposition to her Majesty's Proclamation." The popular leader William Lovett had been one of those arrested, despite his appeals for moderation. He was sentenced to a year's imprisonment. In July, a riot in Liverpool was broken up when the mob "were effectively diffused by the Russian mode of directing on the angry populace a plentiful stream of water from the pipes of a fire engine." The paper called this use of fire hoses "an admirable plan, and one that would be well to pursue in similar cases, though if the water were hot, it might be more effectual."

In another demonstration in Birmingham by the Chartists, a detachment of London police seized the flags and banners of the marchers and tried to arrest the speakers. The crowd of protestors was finally driven from the Bullring, in the city center, by the Military, who used cavalry to inflict many casualties.

In South Wales, a Chartist meeting was held at Cardiff in late July, one month after David and his family had arrived in America. At this meeting, Mr. Frost, "of Newport," was reported as having "regaled about a hundred of the navigators who earn an honest subsistence by daily labor in excavating the mud at the Bute Docks, with a long dissertation upon annual parliaments, universal suffrage, and paying Members (of Parliament) etc." Such talk was an outrage to the editors of *The Cambrian*, who called Frost "a spouting demagogue, attempting to instill in their [the workers] minds the poison of discord and discontent."

The same paper reported that thirty-one people had been found guilty of the earlier rioting at Llanidloes and were duly sentenced, many of them transported to Australia for as much as 15 years. Further riots in the northern English towns of Stockport and Newcastle were reported in September.

As George Crane was regularly sending copies of *The Cambrian* to David in Pennsylvania, the latter must have been well aware of this events and most relieved that he had made the decision to emigrate. The reports of the violence at home certainly must have had no little influence on his decision to remain in his new country even at the end of that first five-year contract.

The Westgate Hotel, Newport, Wales

Despite the antagonism of the newspaper editors towards Chartism and their attempts to belittle it, and despite the speeches given by the great industrialists praising their work in bringing prosperity to the Valleys, the movement kept growing. The authorities continued to live in fear of a general insurrection throughout Britain. The Chartist march on Newport Was planned to take place in early November, 1839. One of the most serious workers' revolts in British history, it resulted in abject failure.

November 9, a full account of the "Great Rising" was given in The Cambrian, a paper that had one day earlier lamented: "It is with extreme grief that we have this week to lay before our readers the particulars of a most atrocious outbreak among the Chartists at Newport." Trouble had been expected for some time, and the military reinforcements from Bristol had been ready and waiting.

According to the newspaper, up to 5,000 rioters "from the hills" (Ebbw Vale; the Varteg, Pontypool, and Dowlais) entered Newport in three columns, one being commanded by John Frost. They marched in an orderly fashion through the streets to the Westgate Hotel where the small group of military waited inside.

Accounts of what happened next vary considerably, but apparently someone in the crowd made the mistake of opening fire on the soldiers, who responded in kind with a shattering volley from the safety of the hotel. Its front ranks decimated, the columns of marchers came to an abrupt halt. Within minutes, amid the smoke from the rifle fire and the screams of the wounded, there was a mad scramble to get away from the square. The crowd fled in panic, leaving over a score dead and many more wounded.

The well-armed troops inside the Westgate Hotel had no difficulty in bringing the pathetic rebellion to a speedy and perhaps totally unexpected conclusion. Despite the hopes and dreams of the many thousands of marchers, who had certainly not anticipated an armed response, the whole affair lasted no more than twenty minutes. Repercussions were to last for a century or more in the political life of South Wales and Monmouthshire.

The Chartist leaders had been among the first to flee. They were reported still at large on November 16 when large rewards were offered by the authorities for the capture of Zephania Williams, Dr. Price, and Jack the Fifer (John Rees).

Zephania Williams was a mineral agent and tavern owner; local hero John Rees had once fought in San Antonio, Texas against the forces of Spain; Dr. Price was regarded as something of an eccentric. On November 23, it was reported that Williams had been taken into custody by Mr. Stockdale, the Superintendent of Cardiff Police; he had been discovered hiding in a sailing vessel outside the sea lock gates.

In the same edition of *The Cambrian* that described the fiasco at Newport, an account is given of a public meeting at Carmarthen to discuss ways to defend the town against the Chartists. It had generally been agreed that in addition to the passive nature of the town, "the citizens were ready and willing to protect themselves, support the Crown, and enforce the laws at all times."

The Carmarthen meeting was declared unnecessary stated a Mr. W. R. Davies, as "there is not a town in her Majesty's dominions more peaceful, more well-disposed, or more loyal." In the same vein, the Merthyr Guardian called the Chartists "traitors." An Anglican minister, Evan Jenkins, stated that Satan was the first Chartist, though he was counteracted in a letter of reply by Ernest Jones who stated that "Christ was the first Chartist, and democracy was the gospel carried into practice."

The Cambrian reported that there was to have been a signal for a general revolt all over the country beginning at Newport, but "the fine fellows of the 45th," chiefly recruited in Ireland and commanded by Lt. Gray, "had gallantly defended the Westgate Inn." (For his part in the affair, Lt. Gray was promoted to Captain). On December 7, the citizens of Newport held a public meeting to thank the gallant 45th for their brave defense of the town — "thus saving it and the whole of England (sic) from rebellion."

The Cambrian also published a second account of the rebellion at Newport, stating that there was every reason to believe the Chartist's "order of the day" was for a simultaneous attack upon Cardiff, Newport and Pontypool on the 5th. By some mistake among the subordinates, the outbreak at Newport had taken place a day too early. Its failure had prevented the general uprising expected to take place throughout the country.

Despite its bitter condemnation of the uprising, its scorn for the leaders, and its relief at its failure, an editorial in *The Cambrian* of January 4, 1840 is worth quoting in full for its feelings regarding both the causes for the growth of the Chartist Movement and for the wrong direction it believed the movement had taken. It certainly reflects the general feelings of those corresponding with David Thomas at that time.

The article states: "Let the public think well of this, and then look back to the acts and proceedings of the Tory administrations, when our prisons were filled with political writers who had committed no offence but that of wounding the feelings of arbitrary ministers, when the laws of the land were suspended by tyrannical enactments, when popular meetings were put down by the sword, and men, women and children massacred cruelly for assembling in peace to petition Parliament — not that we counsel our countrymen to deliver themselves up blindly to the guidance of any ministers. Not at all. Our advice is very different.

We would urge them to have recourse to every means recognized by the constitution for securing their political rights - for obtaining all other privileges that may be justly due them - and for bringing about such reforms as the condition of the times may require. But we contend that these purposes may be accomplished by legal means, without arms, without violence, without bloodshed, simply by the force of reason and public opinion, just as the repeal of the Test and Corporation Act, the abolition of Negro slavery, Catholic Emancipation (the paper neglected to say that there was furious debate over this question in Parliament at the time), and the Reform Bill were achieved."

The editorial mistakenly concluded that if the Chartists were to reflect on these matters, there was little probability that they would again attempt to carry their point by silly and headlong appeals to arms. Its condescending appeal did very little to stop the spread of the movement. It was military force and harsh sentences, not reasoned discourse with a history of being ignored. that made a much bigger impression on the workers.

What *The Cambrian* does not report is that the Chartists were fighting for the rights of all men. Up until the affair at Newport, their behavior, for the most part, had been admirable and entirely within the law. They had co-operated with the Anti-Corn Laws League for the abolition of the bread tax.

The paper also failed to report that the consumption or possession of alcohol was forbidden at all Chartist meetings. The enigmatic and popular Chartist leader Henry Vincent was himself a teatotaller. He believed at the time that the Newport rising had begun merely as a demonstration and had become a rebellion only because government spies had urged the participants to drink. "No riot was intended" he believed, "until some drunken men madly and wickedly fired upon the Westgate Inn."

Covering the trial, *The Cambrian* noted that Mr. Rickard, the defense council, also supported another side of the story, a side that probably reflected the actual events of the so-called insurrection. Rickard said that most of the witnesses who had given their testimony against Frost had themselves been concerned in the transaction, and it might be well to consider how far they might have been influenced by the wish to protect themselves by giving "useful information" and statements worth rewarding.

The jury, continued Rickard, could not believe that the taking of Newport was to be preliminary to a general insurrection, and he would ask, by whom could it be supposed that this was to be effected! "Was it by a famished and hungry mob perishing with cold in a winter's night with arms such as the jury had seen, some of them designated spears, but which were nothing more than rude pieces of iron fixed upon shapeless hedge stakes?

Some of that army had sticks, some muskets, some nothing, and what was it said such an army intended to overthrow - - the ancient and well-compacted Monarchy of this country, supported as it was by many bulwarks, supported as it was by an ancient Peerage, by a wealthy and intelligent aristocracy, by men whose existence was bound up with the preservation of the present state of things, supported by a numerous and loyal army, supported by a gallant navy; above all, supported by a loyal and attached and united people, a very portion of whose national character is the maintenance of the Monarchy — and then to suppose that all these could be struck down by a body of men who were at once scattered through the means of the well-directed fire of a lieutenant, two sergeants and thirty privates!"

The case, Rickart concluded, presented a mass of absurdity which it was necessary to believe before the prisoners could be convicted. This stirring appeal, however, went for naught, as the severe sentences show.

On January 11, 1840 the 54-year old Frost was found guilty of high treason, though the foreman of the jury recommended mercy. On January 18, The

Cambrian reported the findings. Also found guilty were William Jones, and Rees (Jack the Fifer). The paper makes no mention of Zephania Williams at this time, nor of the enigmatic Dr. Price. Scores of others. were reported as being found guilty of taking part in the rebellion.

A week later it was reported that the Bath Chartists had adopted a memorial to the Queen, praying that the sentence passed on Frost and the other leaders may not be carried into effect. Imposing capital punishment on the above guilty authors of rebellion and slaughter, they stated, would be incompatible with the enlightenment of the age. The memorial was accompanied by 9,000 signatures.

Westgate Square, Newport, Wales

Despite the early pleas to the Queen, and the reports of the moral courage of Frost, on January 25 the sentence on Frost, Jones, and Rees was announced. They were "to be taken hence to the place where you came, and be thence drawn on a hurdle to the place of execution, and that each of you be there hanged by the neck until you be dead, and that afterwards the head of each of you shall be severed from his body, and the body of each divided into four quarters, shall be disposed of as her Majesty shall think fit."

In its account of the harsh sentencing, *The Cambrian* had little sympathy for the unfortunate three, describing them as having been involved in what it termed "intended outbreaks, assassinations and Moscowings." All three leaders were stated as having strong minds, but fallacious reasoning powers.

As well as vast outpourings of public sympathy for the three, there was great unrest in industry as well, with a remarkable display of solidarity among most of the workers. The workmen in the Monmouthshire collieries went on strike, the great majority refusing to work alongside the witnesses in the trials.

According to the newspapers, "every remonstrance was used but in vain. Of such importance is it to the proprietors to keep their collieries at work, that they have been obliged to submit to this unwarrantable conduct, and the result is, that these witnesses, through whose endurance the traitors were convicted, are driven from their homes and will be obliged to leave that part of the country."

The Cambrian stated that the trial was noteworthy for the fact that so many witnesses kept so exactly to the depositions at first given — not only to facts but almost in the very same words they at first used to the magistrate. This was accounted for in two ways: first, they were determined to tell the truth. Second, as Welshmen, thinking in that language, though they spoke English well, they naturally put their expressions in the same form over and over again, and confined themselves entirely to the facts, and even to the same words.

According to *The Cambrian*, that these witnesses could understand two languages accounts for their being able to be so verbally accurate in repetition. "If some of the Principality have been unfortunately misled by deep-designing men," the paper continued, "there have been other Welshmen (and those, too, who are most attached to Wales) happily found who have signalized themselves by their upright discharge of duty in defense of their Sovereign and the laws, from Sir Thomas Phillips, a Welshman, the late mayor of Newport, to the Welsh jury on the late trials. It is in times like these that the true metal shows itself, and that the rebel and the coward shrink to nothing, and we are happy to feel that Wales can thus redeem its character."

In his letter of January, 1840, Walters had written of the failure of the great Chartist risings in South Wales. The trials were now over, he wrote, and it was generally believed that the leaders of the Newport Uprising, including Frost, Jones and Rees, "will have to suffer the extreme penalty of the law — thus hanging and beheading, quartering and disposing of their dead bodies."

Like so many of his fellow countrymen, Walters was horrified by these sentences, "The majority here," he continues, "believe that such butchery belongs to heathen practices rather than to a Christian law. If these infatuated have forfeited their lives, it was sufficient that they should be translated to another world in the most decent manner possible . . .this barbarism has no tendency to leave in good affect on the mind of any man."

John Walter's feelings on the trial of the Chartist leaders seems to reflect the general feelings of those who were not directly involved with the movement and who feared the consequences of its growth. It would be foolhardy to challenge the established forces of law and order. For many, there was simply no need for radical movements.

The announcement of the sentences was followed by the drawing up of petitions all over Britain to save the three popular Chartist leaders. In Swansea, 2,543 signatures were collected. In Merthyr alone, there were 15,786 signatures to release Frost, whose death sentence, along with those of his companions, was commuted to life imprisonment in Australia.

One of the leaders of the rebellion, Dr. Price, who had been organizing the supply of arms for the marchers, had managed to escape capture. With a large fee on his head, he had been helped aboard ship disguised as a woman by the very police officer sent to prevent his escape! Price remained in France for a time before returning to Wales.

In *The Cambrian*, John Frost was described as the leader of the Chartists, between 50 and 60 years of age "and of a quiet, respectable appearance." Popular at Newport, where he was a linen draper, he had been elected to the Town Council and recommended to be one of the Borough magistrates, which recommendation was ratified by Lord John Russell.

According to the paper, ever on the side of the English authorities, Frost's subsequent political conduct, however, "became so violent, his consenting to be chosen to the National Convention {of Chartists}, that he was removed from the magistry, which only increased his enmity to the Government; and he threw himself into the arms of Chartists." Frost's wife was also reported to be Chairwoman of the Female Association of Chartists at Newport.

During the trial, *The Cambrian* reported Frost as having seven children, one son having emigrated to America. The paper stated that all the prisoners except Frost were loud in their complaints of being manacled. He alone maintained his firmness and composure and "presented his wrist to be handcuffed without making a single observation." Frost was also reported as devoting a large portion of the day to the arrangement of his defense in a calm and perfectly businesslike manner.

A portrait of Frost was available for sale: "Politicians and patrons of art are equally interested in a publication now issuing from the press," stated The Cambrian, "being the only authentic portrait of the Chartist leader, Frost, taken at the time of the passing of the awful sentence of the law." The attributes of moral courage and physical endurance are strongly depicted in this unrivalled work of art." The notice continued, "The immense sale which we understand this production has met with, can alone account for the very moderate charge of one shilling at which it is sold."

In the meantime, two Welsh Chartist newspapers were published: the *Udgorn Cymru* and the *Merthyr Advocate and Free Press*. Meetings continued throughout the 1840's and many Chartists contributed to a land plan by forming a co-operative society. Others turned to trade unionism to fulfill their hopes.

Despite the dismal failure at Newport and other towns and cities in Britain, the spirit of Chartism was not yet finished in the land. The twenty-minute rebellion had stirred the conscience of the nation despite the ridicule and contempt heaped upon it in the national newspapers. Unfortunately great unrest all over Europe in the late 1840's meant that the British government was extremely suspicious of anything that reeked of socialism, and the Press continued to denigrate all their activities, calling them" seditionists, ragamufins, demagogues, and spouters of treason."

Robert Owen, the great reformer and visionary, who had attempted to improve factory conditions, shorten hours of work, educate factory children, and who had set up a system of 'villages of co-operation' first in New Lanark, Scotland and later in New Harmony, Indiana, was labelled in the press as "a lunatic."

After serving some time in Australia, Frost managed to visit his son in the United States, where he stayed for two years. In 1856, he came back to South Wales on a conditional pardon, to be given a hero's welcome. Still active in denouncing the Government, he spoke at a public meeting in Merthyr in 1857. His pioneering work along with that of the others who had sacrificed so much was not entirely in vain.

By 1858 the Chartist Movement had faded. That year an act was passed declaring that property qualifications were no longer necessary for Parliament, and thus the first great democratizing point of the Charter had been conceded by the Government. In any case, as the infamous Corn Laws had been repealed in 1846 and bread was a little cheaper, people felt less inclined to armed revolt.

The Great Reform Bill of 1867 finally brought the Chartist movement to an end, for in that year nearly one million voters were added to the register, almost a doubling of the electorate. Forty-five new seats were created and the vote given to many workingmen in the towns and cities.

Chapter Ten

More Troubled Times in Wales

Despite all his fears about the Chartists, writing from the Ynyscedwyn Works in his letter to David Thomas dated September 10, 1840, George Crane had been very optimistic about the future of the iron industry in South Wales; he mentioned the large orders then coming in to Ynyscedwyn. His optimism, however, was not borne out by subsequent events.

According to contemporary articles in *The Cambrian*, reductions in the iron trade and the consequent discharge of large numbers of men had produced "an extent and degree of distress among the working classes that was truly affecting." Gangs of unemployed, many of them Irish, roamed throughout the South Wales coalfield, looking for work and causing trouble. They found little of the former, lots of the latter.

The depression in the industry meant that, in December, 1840, the South Wales iron masters agreed on measures to save themselves from what they considered to be ruin arising from the low prices of iron. They agreed to diminish the make of iron by one fourth for 6 months. Accordingly, a number of furnaces were to be blown out on December 1, and one fourth of all the workmen were to be discharged.

On December 10, a letter from Merthyr Tydfil to *The Cambrian* noted that these resolutions had been put into effect, and the result had involved all the densely populated districts of South Wales "in a most frightful state of confusion and terror." The iron masters had also been gradually lessening the men's wages, commencing with one shilling in the pound, which they then reduced by two shillings and ultimately two shillings and sixpence. The workmen, finding that they could not support themselves and their families on such reduced wages, resolved to strike.

The strike began at Rhymney Iron Works, and men from there were sent to other works to request ("compel" according to The Cambrian) the men to join in the work stoppage. Dr. Thomas, it was reported, "our very active magistrate" popular in the district "despite his being a Tory," immediately called out the whole new police force.

In defiance, the strikers marched to the nearby towns of Tredegar, Nantyglo and Dowlais where all the civil forces and the military were put in a state of readiness. At Rhymney the furnaces were extinguished, "leaving a desert silence reigning where were once all the bustle, hurry and hum of a busy, active life."

According to the paper, men wanted their iron masters or their government to relieve their "oppressive, wretched, and starving conditions." Again, however, the massive appeal came to naught. Neither the government or the captains of industry were sufficiently interested in alleviating the pitiful condition of the iron workers who were humiliatingly forced to end their strike and return to work, having gained nothing but lower wages and starvation. In many instances, they also suffered loss of their jobs to others moving into the area from Northern England or Ireland. The newcomers, especially the poor Irish, would not hesitate to work at the lower wages.

In an editorial on December 17, *The Cambrian*, ultra-conservative as it was, in analyzing the reasons for the great Chartist uprising at Newport earlier the previous year and the subsequent attempt at a general strike, showed a surprisingly sympathetic side when it summarized the situation:

"Never since the close of the great European war in 1816 has the state of the country been more alarming than at present" it reported. "Hundreds are starving, thousands are thrown out of employment, and thousands are forced to accept a level of wages which barely keep body and soul together and which can only be paid out of the decreasing capital of the masters."

The paper continued: "The literally total extinction of the iron trade, coupled with the simultaneous extinction of their forges by the English, Scotch and Welsh miners, must throw countless multitudes upon the poor rates in the course of the winter and reduce to the verge of a dangerous despair a hardy population — who have already given proof to the affrighted world of their desperate courage and benighted ignorance — despite the ridicule with which some minds have covered the defeat of Frost and his rioters by a handful of military, we must consider the state of mind which could impel men to rise in open rebellion, as an awful result of pressure and despair."

What was termed "yet another grave menace to the people of Britain" was reported in *The Cambrian* in April, 1840. As in so many times past, a new religious movement had come into the Valleys to give solace and comfort to many who did not know where else to turn. It was not welcomed by the newspapers or by those in authority. This was the arrival of the Mormon missionaries from the United States.

On May 4, readers were warned of being duped by the "Mormonites,'" who would delude them away from Wales "to a strange country — a new Jerusalem on the banks of the Ohio — where on their arrival, they will find themselves deserted by the swindlers of this knavish sect who have seduced them away, and will have nothing left but to die in poverty and lay their bones in a foreign and neglected grave."

The dire warning seems to have had little effect, however, for later in the year the same paper reported that a group of 70 Welsh people had emmigrated to the United States as newly-converted Mormons. *The Cambrian* called them "ignorant fanatics." The report went on to state with great satisfaction: "... and we see by an article in the *Toronto Patriot* that the arch imposter Smith, the originator of his extraordinary delusion, has been apprehended and is now in gaol." (Note: as late as 1990, the U.S. Census reported a higher percentage of people with Welsh ancestry living in Utah than in any other state).

The newspapers carried other warnings, equally as dire. In December, it carried the dreadful news that smallpox had caused upwards of 30,000 deaths in Britain in the past two years. Parents of all children were advised to take notice of the provisions made by the new act of the 4th and 5th year of the reign of Queen Victoria, for the extension of vaccination with the cow pox, and the prevention of the spread of smallpox.

Every child was to be vaccinated when six weeks old, unless "it be delicate or suffering from disease." In that case, stated the report, "the operation could be deferred for a week or two." If smallpox was to be found in any neighborhoods, all were to be vaccinated without delay, even infants a few days after birth. The Act of Parliament had made it an offense punishable by one month's imprisonment, "for any person by any means to produce the disease of smallpox."

If that punishment seems severe, it was an age when punishments were severe indeed. We have seen the sentences passed on Frost and his companions, only commuted after impassioned pleas to the Queen from thousands upon thousands of her loyal citizens, and then only to banishment to Australia for life.

In Wales, *The Cambrian* reported that Philip Bevan, for stealing a small piece of soap from his master, was sentenced to six weeks' hard labor including one week in solitary confinement. In another case, one woman was given a similar sentence for stealing a small piece of cheese from her employer. In a lighter vein, early in 1840 there was a trial reported at Caernarfon, in North Wales, where a man was accused of seducing a farmer's daughter.

The newspaper account reports that "a great number of young men were produced for the defense as witnesses." Apparently, they had all courted the woman (who was then with child) after "the strange and absurd custom of the country (bundling)." The trial judge, Mr. Justice Williams commented on the "perilous" Welsh custom of courting in bed.

At the trial, reported the paper, it was not proved that the father of the 26 year-old plaintiff had not shown that care and caution in the custody of his daughter which Welshmen of his condition should have taken. The verdict was for the plaintiff and the damages were assessed at 20 pounds and costs. The practice of bundling or "courting in bed" seems to be very much a part of life in nineteenth century rural Wales.

The age saw very little in the way of social justice. Conditions in industry were frightful. A Royal Commission in 1842 was set up to report on the employment of children and young persons in British industry, especially to examine their working conditions. An important part of the report to the Royal Commission (which was published in six volumes) was specifically related to the Ynyscedwyn Iron Works and the nearby furnaces at Ystalyfera.

Some miners were employing children as young as three years of age to hold their candles for them as they cut the coal. From early morning until late at night, these children worked alongside their fathers, until "when exhausted with fatigue, they cradled upon the coals." Other children were regularly taken along to work at the age of five; the report showed that 17 out of 30 children in 6 Welsh coal pits were between the ages of 5 and 9.

It was the task of some of the children to draw loaded wagons. Young boys and girls crawled naked on their hands and feet, in total blackness, pulling wagons of 2 to 5 hundredweight. They buckled large leather straps around their waists to which chains were attached to the wagons. Other children were employed as early as seven years of age to keep open the air-way doors in the mines.

At 10 years of age, other children took care of the horses deep down in the mine shafts. The usual hours for these child laborers were from 6 am until 6 p.m. with half an hour off to eat some dry bread for dinner and perhaps some potatoes and a small piece of fat bacon for supper.

Despite these appalling conditions, there was no rest for the workers on Sundays, for the blast furnaces had to be kept in operation to save any detriment in the quality of iron. At the Ynyscedwyn Works, at the time of Thomas' departure for America, there were over 500 adults and 60 children, of whom 28 were under the age of 13 and five were young girls.

In working the mines of iron ore in patches, where the ore was found a few feet from the surface, the girls were frequently employed in assisting the workmen. They were called patch girls, described as leading a sort of half-savage life. "Hardy and exposed to all kinds of weather, they work as hard as the men, from whom they differ but little in dress and quite equal in grossness."

Even as late as 1890, the *London Iron and Steel Trades Journal* reported that the great obstacle to tinplate making on a large scale in the United States was the entire absence of cheap female labor, so necessary in the industry, "and so abundant in Wales."

The 1842 Commission's report was that it was desirable for children to stay in school to acquire at least the rudiments of a good education until the age of 10 or 12. The report, and others like it were much criticized by the factory owners, coal owners, and iron masters but they did lead, eventually, to social and electoral reforms that were reflected in subsequent Factory Acts.

The Acts that followed the Commission were long overdue. Down to 1824, it had been a punishable offense for mechanics to form societies for the purpose of peacefully endeavoring to raise their wages. It was not until 1871, in fact, that trade unions were legalized in Britain. In a speech in The House of Commons in 1850, a Mr. Huskisson stated that "If capital had not a fair remuneration here (in Britain), it would seek for it in America. To give it a fair remuneration, the price of labour must be kept down."

Acts of Parliament designed to protect children and to shorten the hours of labor met with vigorous opposition from the iron masters and colliery owners. As late as 1875 the London Fortnightly Review stated that "for more than four hundred years it had been the settled policy of British legislators that it was a crime for a workman to seek higher wages."

At a Woolen Trade Banquet held in New York City in 1870, the President of the Chamber of Commerce stated that he had seen in the iron mills of Wales "young girls, with their heavy shoes and short, woolen dresses, wheeling iron, cinder, coals, etc., at night, among the half-naked puddlers, doing the work done by men and boys in our mills, and receiving for a week's wages what we [American workers] receive for a day."

Some time in 1850, it was pointed out by a visitor that at Brynmawr, in Southeast Wales, "nearly every family was in the employment of Mr. Bailey, the iron master. The town reeks with dirt; there are no lamps or effective drainage; and not the slightest step has been taken to improve the mental or moral condition of the violent and vicious community."

The writer continued, "Neither church nor school has been established by those who employ the people or own the land; and the only step that has been taken for their benefit is that of establishing — a police station!" The major employer of the workers at Brynmawr was the same Mr. Bailey who had so eloquently praised his own efforts in bringing prosperity to his district.

As we have seen earlier, one easily available solace was drink. The British workingman drinks, wrote one American author at the time, because British statesmen and manufacturers offer to him the public house as something better than his cheerless home. Public houses were warm, even comfortably furnished. For a few pennies spent on drink, they offered a temporary refuge for those who lived in little more than hovels.

Yet slowly conditions were beginning to improve. In its edition for March 25, 1876, *Ryland's Own Trade Circular* stated that the British people were "gradually coming to a more reasonable range of prices, through concessions which have been wrung from ironworkers and colliers."

For many, these concessions were too little and too late. No wonder so many of David Thomas's colleagues and friends in Wales wished to join him in Pennsylvania. In late 1840, his own mother wrote that she was so badly off, she needed David to send her some money "rightaway.". The letter was in English, reflecting a Welsh speaker's eccentric spellings of the unfamiliar language.

Strangely enough, the letter does not mention the recent serious damage caused by a major fire at Windsor Castle which was as much national news as

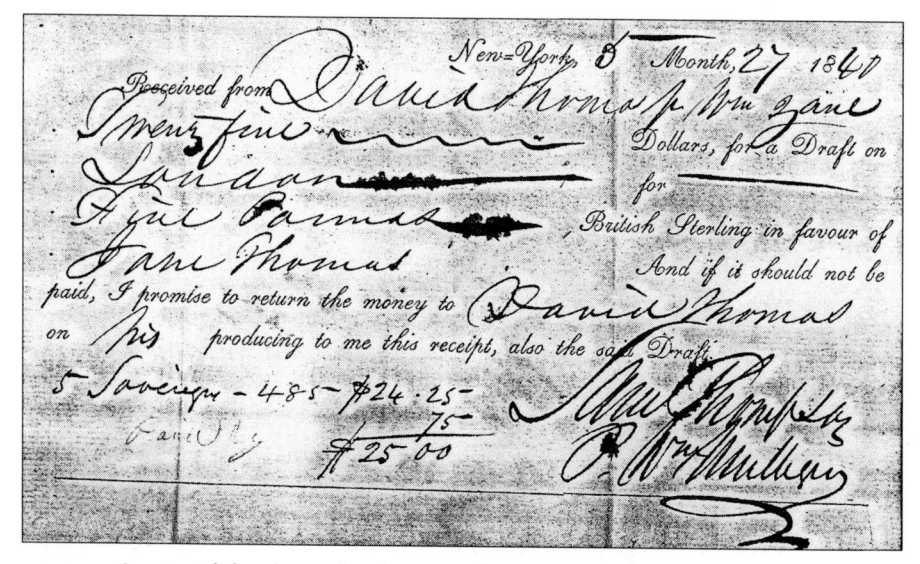

A copy of the cheque for five pounds sent to Jane by David Thomas dated June 27, 1840

a similar fire over one hundred and fifty years later. It had certainly been reported in the major newspapers of the day, including *The Cambrian*. Mrs. Thomas does mention the sadness felt at the death of the American President (William Henry Harrison), as well as her concern about the missing trans-Atlantic liner, co-incidentally named the *President*.

Earlier in the year, George Crane had written that many of Thomas's former friends had gone to London to see Queen Victoria get married "of which event," he stated, "they are not a little proud." Jane Thomas's letter, however, is mostly concerned with family matters. Thomas's sister Jane had just given birth to a fine son. David's mother Jane is thankful for the money that Thomas has sent from America. She refers to the iron works "hear" (in South Wales) being very slow and everything being very expensive.

In this letter, David was told that at the Neath Abbey Works men had been reduced to working only three-quarters of each day. Meat was selling at 6 pence and 9 pence a pound; butter was 18 pence a pound. Hopkin Hopkins, one of the workers at Ynyscedwyn, and a tenant of Jane Thomas, was having trouble paying his debts, but Jane didn't want him to go to the law, as she believed the lawyers would get everything and "no one will be the better for it."

Yet not all the news that arrived in letters or reported in contemporary literature was unpleasant. Most interesting is the fact that, in a letter written by Patrick Moir Crane to David Thomas in February, 1840, sent via Bristol for the Atlantic passage on the Great Western, there is a printed letter heading:

"To avoid the surcharge of One Penny each way, under the new regulations of the General Post-Office, the Ynyscedwin Iron Company will be obligated to their friends to post-pay any letters to Ynyscedwin Iron Works, on the understanding that, they on their part, will post-pay all letters which may be sent in return."

This is the first letter from the iron works upon which such a heading appears. The new regulations of the Post-Office to which Patrick Moir Crane refers had been in the offing for a long time. We have seen how many of the letters sent to David Thomas were written to utilize every single inch of paper available. Before the Postal reforms, letters were very expensive; they were priced by weight. Not only that, but it seemed that each postal district set its own rates.

During the early 1830's, led by Rowland Hill, there had consequently been great demands for reform of the whole British Postal system, with its chaos of conflicting local regulations. In mid-March, 1839, a report of the Committee on Postage detailed the discussion in which it was decided to introduce uniform postal rates. The committee stated that "the present high rates were a grievous tax on the poor; new rates would let the poor avail themselves of the Post-Office — and though their contributions might be small individually, yet, taking their number into consideration, the aggregate amount would be most important."

On March 30, 1839 it was reported in *The Cambrian* that Mr. Hill's plan of the reduction of the postage had received a trial in Gloucestershire that resulted in more than forty times the usual number of letters being posted. On April 6, writing of the success at Gloucestershire (a border county) of the new postage, *The Cambrian* advised its readers to press for the same system to be put into use in Wales. "The inhabitants of South Wales should be on the move," it stated, "as no proposition, in our humble opinion, was ever better sustained by reason and sound policy."

The same edition commented on the new Post Office regulations that had come into effect in March. Postmasters were advised that "letters to and from North America, conveyed by her Majesty's packets, having been reduced to the uniform rate of one shilling single and two shillings double — you will in future charge that rate upon such letters without adding any charge for inland postage."

On May 11, 1839 it was reported that the Mercantile Committee had recommended Mr. Hill's plan as a whole and for the immediate reduction of postage universally to one penny. A public meeting was to be called very shortly to discuss the matter. The arrival of the *South America* and the *Hibernia* from the United States, reported on July 13, brought the news "that the universal feeling throughout Great Britain in favor of cheap postage has communicated itself to the people of the United States."

On July 20, *The Cambrian* reported that "a resolution pledging The House of Commons to adopt penny postage was passed last night." The new scheme was to begin on January 1, 1840. On February 7, 1840 the same newspaper published an article about the penny post.

Cheap postage, it stated, will prove of immense benefit to the men employed in the iron works of Glamorganshire and Monmouthshire. Many of them had families residing in Carmarthenshire to whom they sent a sovereign or half sovereign per week. This used to cost one shilling and six pence under the old system "besides four pence for sending the letter to the town in the iron master's bag." At that time, the article reported, there was no Post Office at Tredegar, Nantyglo, Beaufort, Ebbw Vale or Brynmawr "though these places contained 30,000 inhabitants."

On the first day of May, 1840, the letter stamps came into operation. The Cambrian reported that this was the first day of the complete carrying into effect of Rowland Hills's plan. Just as in neighboring Gloucestershire, the increase in the numbers of letters sent daily in South Wales increased forty times. On a more humorous note, on August 20th, the same newspaper carried the news that the gum of the new postage was extremely tempting to mice and black beetles: serious losses were being incurred by postmasters placing sheets of stamps within the reach of "these remorseless epicures."

It is not difficult to conjecture just how precious were David's letters home and why John Walters and others had saved space in their letters to America by writing across the lines. The cheaper rates meant that letters to David from some of his Welsh friends no longer had to be written across and down the same side of the paper.

Because of his work in reducing the costs of mailing letters, Sir Rowland Hill became so revered in Wales that the organizers of the 1863 Eisteddfod wished to honor his memory in song. In the meantime, however, the mixture of Welsh and English in the letters to David, however, reveal what was happening to the Welsh language.

Chapter Eleven

The Question of the Welsh Language.

George Crane was right to foresee that David Thomas and his family would not return to live in Wales at the expiration of that first five-year contract. In fact, David made only one visit home, to see his aged and ailing mother (who outlived her husband by twenty years). Thanks to men such as Thomas, his new country was fast becoming the most powerful industrial nation on earth, and he was taking a major role in that total experience.

At the same time, there were great changes taking place in Britain as a whole and in Wales in particular. The success of the American colonies, in asserting their independence from the English Crown, had its repercussions in Wales, where a new desire for recognition of its separate identity had made itself felt in the 1790's.

Wales had been politically part of England since the Acts of Union of 1536. Its legal system had been made to conform to that of England much earlier. Edward lst had convened a parliament at Rhuddlan, in North Wales, for that purpose in 1284. Two years earlier, the last native-born Prince of Wales, Llywelyn ap Gruffudd had been killed fighting English armies intending to put a stranglehold on his beloved country. His brother Dafydd, attempting to continue the struggle, had been put to death a year later.

A major rebellion led by Owain Glyndŵr to restore independence in the early years of the 15th century was crushed by the English Crown when the tripartite alliance of Glyndŵr, Hotspur, and Mortimer fell apart. It was also then that dreams of nationhood practically came to an end. After Union in 1536, Wales lived under an alien political system, forced to play a subordinate role as an integral part of the kingdom of England (and later, Great Britain).

After Britain's relatively peaceful conversion to Protestantism in the age of the Tudors, constant threats of invasion from Spain (and sometimes from Scotland and France), kept the people of Wales closely allied to their fellow islanders in England. Both nations feared of a return to what was considered a morally and spiritually bankrupt Church of Rome. From 1588 on, Welsh people had their own Protestant Bible, written in their own language. Peacefully managing their own affairs, they were relatively content with the situation.

A sense of a shared religious destiny slowly but surely integrated itself into the minds of both English and Welsh so that they began to think of themselves as also sharing a common British heritage. This sense of a common heritage was certainly cemented by the union of Scotland with England in 1701. From that time on, the modern nation of Great Britain can be said to have begun.

Yet the survival of the Welsh language meant the survival of a nation that was reminded of its unique and separate traditions. Unlike the majority of the people of Scotland, the Welsh persisted in holding on to their ancient Celtic language. In 1730, Lord Raymond proposed in the House of Lords that all parliamentary proceedings be translated into Welsh "so as to deepen his people's attachment to it." The proposal was dismissed as ludicrous by the Scottish Duke of Argyll. But the survival of the Welsh language meant the survival of a nation that was reminded of its unique and separate traditions in the waning years of the 18th century.

There is a Welsh expression that translates as "The best Welshmen live outside Wales," and it is noticeable that most of the advocates of Welsh nationhood lived outside Wales, in London. In the 1770's, in his emotional addresses, visionary Edward Williams (Iolo Morganwg) reminded his fellow London-Welshmen not only what it was to belong to the ancient Celtic race. He advised them what they themselves could do to ensure that Welsh traditions became known and handed down to posterity, even if some of these traditions had to be newly invented!

There was also the stirring effect of Sir William Jones's dramatic address of 1792 (also to the London Welsh Society) that announced the discovery of America by Prince Madoc three hundred years before Columbus. Jones praised of the so-called Welsh Indians, the Mandans, who were "a free and distinct people...who have preserved their liberty, language and some trace of their religion to this very day."

Though subsequent events did not bear out the truth of William Jones's theories, and Elizabeth Thomas's ideas about the "Welshness" of Pennsylvania were far too imaginative, if not ill-informed, Welsh people were certainly prominent in the new republic. But at least her husband was right; it is known that at least five signers of the Declaration of Independence were Welsh-Americans and there may have been more than twice that number who could claim Welsh or part-Welsh descent.

It was Sir William Jones, while working in India, who had discovered the connection between the Celtic languages and Sanskrit, in which the sacred writings of India are written. His work gave to the Welsh language a long history and an ancestry of which all Welshmen and women could be proud.

When the French Revolution followed the one in America, the London Welsh, in a state of euphoria, seeing some kind of hope for a sense of Welsh nationhood as well, revived the long-moribund Eisteddfod. They wanted to take the annual festival of poetry and music that dated back many centuries, and make it a national affirmation. It was first necessary to give the ceremony a sense of dignity clothed in some kind of pageantry.

As there was sadly lacking a coherent body of Welsh cultural traditions, Iolo Morganwg invented them, along with the elaborate and fanciful ceremony conducted at the Eisteddfod. Some of these were entirely unknown to the Welsh people at the time, but intermittently augmented and effectively managed, have become an integral and much-loved part of the event ever since, eagerly looked forward to and well-attended.

It was Williams, a stonemason from the Vale of Glamorgan, who invented the Gorsedd, the guild of bards that today plays such a prominent role in Welsh cultural affairs and which is responsible for the holding of the annual National Eisteddfod. He also called for a national library for Wales, and a national museum.

Encouraged by such efforts, by the turn of the century, the first serious democratic and popular movements in Wales had begun, and the Welsh language grew in stature and strength along with them. Ironically, it was the preponderance of Welsh speakers in Wales that caused the Government to question and to reform its system of education into a purely English-language model in the 1840's.

In George Crane's letter to David Thomas dated September 10, 1840, he mentioned that a new school for infants was being built at Ystradgynlais. The work people, had "at two most agreeable meetings, authorized us to deduct 6 pence per month from each man's wages towards our own advances for a building fund, and 3 pence a month towards a stipend for the schoolmaster and mistress. By their exertions, too, they have managed to increase the Sunday School perhaps to 180 or 200."

Crane continues, perhaps alluding to the dislike towards him he felt from many of his workers, "We are now doing all we can, and you will not consider that I am the least useful Saxon whoever came into Wales." But as far as the British government was concerned, local efforts like those of Crane at Ystradgynlais were not enough; too many in Wales were not learning English fast enough, for one thing; and for another, too many were not even learning it at all.

Among its very negative reports on the status of education in Wales, the Royal Commission of 1842 had noted that some Welsh boys employed at mines in Breckonshire (as the county was then called) were learning to read English at Sunday schools, but that they could speak only Welsh.

Because of such findings of the Commission, it was demanded in Parliament that an inquiry be conducted into the state of education in Wales, especially into the means afforded to the laboring classes of acquiring a knowledge of the English tongue. This led to another Royal Commission, conducted in 1847, which was to have a lasting effect on the cultural and political life of Wales.

The detailed report, in three volumes and bound in blue covers, became known as the *Blue Books*. According to all subsequent accounts, the three lawyers appointed to conduct the survey were young, inexperienced members of the Anglican Church with no special experience in education, who did not have any understanding of the Welsh language; nor, it seems, did they understand Welsh non-conformity in religious matters. Bright, intelligent and well-read Welsh speaking children were unable to understand the questions put to them in the English language, and this was seen by the surveyors as nothing more than sheer ignorance.

Such were the kind of inspectors chosen to investigate the state of education in a country that was mostly Welsh-speaking and Nonconformist. We have to remember that even as late as World War 1, over a million inhabitants of Wales spoke the Welsh language, the great majority of these as their first language for every day communication. As late as 1921, in fact, there were 929, 824 people who spoke Welsh, of whom 40 percent lived in Glamorganshire. The inspectors sent to examine the schools in Wales knew no Welsh!

When the *Blue Books* report finally appeared, it lamented the deplorable condition of the too few schools, the unqualified teachers, lack of supplies and text books, and the irregular attendance of the children. The report attributed all these, along with dirtiness, laziness, ignorance, superstition, promiscuity and immorality to Nonconformity (that is the practice of religion outside the established church) and to the Welsh language, making many of its speakers feel ashamed and embarrassed.

The effects of the controversy thus stirred up lasted for a century or more; it certainly did much to bolster the position of those who agreed with much of the report. One drastic remedy — the consequent imposition of English-only Board schools over much of Wales did a great deal to hasten the general decline of the Welsh language.

In the Board schools, the "Welsh Not" rule was imposed, with severe penalties for speaking Welsh, including the wearing of the infamous wooden board around one's neck. On the other hand, according to many, what was regarded as "the treachery of the Blue Books" did much to revive national sentiment and patriotism and brought about a spirited defense of Welsh as a language of the people.

On April 10, 1840, another letter was sent to her son by David's mother. It is in English. She mentions the very poor harvest and the fact that a supply of hay had to be brought in from England to keep the cattle alive. From Jane's subsequent letters, there is reason to believe that this letter was dictated by her and written by someone else — a Welsh friend who knew some English.

At the time, statistics show that 35 percent of the population of Wales could not read or write at all. About half the population could read or write Welsh "imperfectly," and only about 9 percent could read and write well in either language. Coming from a farming family, it is very unlikely that Jane could write well in Welsh; she certainly could not have written in English.

When the Thomas family first arrived in America, even David's wife knew no English at all. But the use of English in Wales was increasing in the larger cities such as Swansea, where *The Cambrian*, the largest and most influential newspaper, founded in 1804, primarily for the maritime industry, was published entirely in that language.

In the 1830's, letters written almost daily show there was intense debate raging as to the future of the Welsh language and Welsh institutions at that time. Then, as now, many people in Wales were questioning the value of retaining the old language. Both sides were given expression in letters to The Cambrian.

Tied up with the language question, of course, was the fate of the National Eisteddfod, which at the time was conducted in both English and Welsh. On August 1, 1840, notice was given of the Eisteddfod and procession of the Bards to be be held at Swansea.

The newspaper goes on to state: "The Druidic Eisteddfod about to take place in this town, will, we have no doubt, reward the spirited exertions of its originators with the success they merit - - we hope that ladies and gentlemen will assist by their presence on the occasion, in order to wipe off the reproach, that it is impossible to rouse the metropolis of Wales [Swansea] from the apathy which it labors under, with regard to anything connected with Wales and Welshmen." It seems that only the London Welsh were taking their language and the question of Welsh nationhood seriously.

Another closely related problem to that of language and the Eisteddfod was that of the appointment to Welsh bishoprics. As early as 1764, a Welsh poet Evan Evans had spoken that he was looked upon by Bishops in Wales "with and evil eye because I dare have any affection for my country, language, and antiquities, which in their opinion had better been lost and forgotten." Evans continued, "As Bishops we have only grasping self-seekers, who endeavour to deprive us of the light of God's word in our own language."

The deplorable situation hadn't changed by mid-nineteenth century. On August 15, 1840, a letter in *The Cambrian* from a Welsh clergyman remarked on the Welsh Sees being all filled by Englishmen or English-speaking Welshmen. "In the place where I was educated" [St. David's Theological College, Lampeter] the clergyman writes, "intended be it remarked, for the Welsh Church, I was never required to read, to speak, or to write one line in the language of my country; and those educated with me ridiculed the idea of ever studying that language, as they could go to _____ to study Welsh, and get a certificate stating their competency."

Over one hundred and fifty years later, Welsh newspapers were still reporting the filling of positions in the Welsh Church with English clergymen or English-speaking Welsh clergymen, there being a shortage of Welsh speakers entering the profession.

This defense of the language was followed by a letter in a completely different vein on September 5. In this, the writer blames the Welsh language for what he calls the country's moral turpitude: "I cherish the hope," he writes," that I may yet see the day when Wales, no longer the seat of barbarity and heathenism, will herself take a fit position (from which she has so long been excluded) in moral literature and science. It may be asked, how was Wales set aside from that past, which is the glory and pride of every other nation.

"The answer is simple," the letter continues: "She is bound with fetters as yet indissoluble which she seems to hug with increasing tenacity — namely her language — the Welshman is a fool, his language is his folly — he prefers others to enjoy his goods, he prefers being laughed at as a puppet in Druidic processions and Bardic Eisteddfodau." The writer wishes to see the disappearance of that language, "without which act, we can never hope to be recognized otherwise than as simple, good-natured, honest barbarians."

This astonishing letter was written at the same time that Lady Charlotte Guest was making known to the world some of the glories of Welsh literature through her translations of the *Mabinogion*, still being undertaken during the late 1830's and eventually published until 1846. Sadly enough, that such letters were still being written to newspapers in Wales in the 1990's shows only too well the success of the British government's attempts to wipe out the language that date back to the Acts of Union of Henry VIII.

On December 21 a long letter appeared praising Welsh literature in answer to an earlier one that stated that Wales would be most materially benefited by the substitution of the English tongue for her native language. Though the writer of the second letter agrees, stating "every day we have fresh confirmation of the soundness of that opinion, by the progressive spread of English and the very perceptible desire of the Welsh," in literature, however, he believes things are very different. Despite the great progress of the English language in Wales, he states, most of the inhabitants take a pride in knowing at least two languages, and so far as they may be considered superior to the mere Englishman.

"By acquiring the knowledge of English," the writer continues, "the natives of Wales do not, with the exception of an occasional *Dic Sion Dafydd* (a term roughly equivalent of that of Uncle Tom in the U.S.), relinquish their own language, and we can safely assert that the Welsh language is cultivated, read, and appreciated, in a two-fold degree more in our days that it was 50 years ago."

In proof of this, the writer then states, "there is scarcely a town (in Wales) of 1500 population without its printing establishment in full activity, from which are continually issuing works of merit, both in original compositions and translations of the best works of other nations."

Sporadic attempts to give the Welsh language more recognition were taking place on purely local levels. The December 18, 1840 edition of *The Cambrian* contained a petition to the Queen from the Welsh inhabitants of Liverpool (who numbered over 50,000) asking for a new order of knighthood in honor of Wales and two Welsh professorships at English universities (Oxford and Cambridge). There were several replies. One of these suggested that there should be scholarships initiated for Welsh people instead.

Another writer, using the expression "as poor as Taffy" was amused by a proposal to have the infant Prince of Wales instructed in the Welsh language. He wrote that the prince, by trying to pronounce the Welsh "ll" or "ch," would be perceived as having spasmodic affections of the bronchial tubes "that would lead to quinsy or some terrible disease of the lungs and jugulum and would alarm everyone."

The writer goes on to ask readers to consider the roars of laughter in the House of Commons when the budget of the day includes the following items: "Three thousand pounds per annum for teaching His royal highness Welsh, making leek broth, and the national mode of eating it." The idea, he continued, was revolting, "like trying to cram a calf with logic: nature forbids it."

The same kind of silly arguments appeared in Wales's newspapers in the late 1960's when Prince Charles was being taught Welsh at Aberystwyth University. Newspapers in Wales in the 1990's were still filled with letters and articles almost daily as to the merits of continuing the Welsh language in the schools, of teaching it to newcomers, and of the relevance of Welsh in the modern world. Even now, as then, there seems to be no end of the argument.

It is worth noting that Queen Victoria had been in favor of keeping the language alive. In a statement to Lord Landsdowne in 1849, she advocated that "Welsh should be taught in Wales as well as English."

Jane Thomas wrote another letter to her son on May 18, 1840. This also was entirely in English but in a different hand from that used in her earlier letter. In the second letter, even the date is written as Mayth 18 — a usage typical of a Welsh-speaking person. The first two sentences will give some idea of the degree of the writer's lack of proficiency in the English language:

"I have the obertunity with our Sevoure to answer your kinnd and welcom letter once more in hoping theus few lines will find you and your wife and chirldren in good states of health as it leaves us at preasant except myself.... I have had a littel axcident my foot did slip by the Door I fell down and strain of my leg and I am verrey bad my dear son I have send 3 letters to you befoare and had not recved only one leter of the 3..." Then, at the end of her letter, Jane asks her son to "Place to writ the next letter in Enlish."

Perhaps Jane was going to share her son's letters with some of her English friends; it is difficult to tell why a native Welsh speaker would make such a request. Her daughter-in-law, Elizabeth, was, of course, learning English in America, and more and more people in the Swansea valley were beginning to use it. George Crane still knew no Welsh, and he often stopped at Ty Llwyd in his brougham to chat over the hedge with Jane and to discuss the latest happenings in Allentown.

David used to send information to Crane to pass on to his mother as well as sending her money from time to time. Letters from overseas were a priceless possession, to be shared with family and friends and possibly with some of the men who had worked with Thomas. This is only a guess, of course, but maybe Jane wanted to be part of the new movement by so many in South Wales at the time, in the face of so many English-speaking immigrants, to discard the language of their ancestors.

There were certainly thousands of newcomers into the valleys of South Wales whose very numbers prevented their absorption into a totally Welsh culture and whose retention of the English language had a profound effect upon the whole of Welsh culture and social life right up to the present day.

In 1832, when work was being extended on the Brecon Forest Tramroad, one of the engineers was the Englishman John Brunton. He called his Welsh workers "members of a lazy, primitive, uncivilized race, having a great dislike to Englishmen — Saxons as they called them." He also said that among the Welsh "petty thefts were common, and they found the English fair game." Brunton complained that he had to learn enough Welsh "to make Taffy understand what I wanted" (at the time, the whole valley was a monoglot Welsh community, with "even the parson having only a very imperfect command of English").

Despite the strength of the language in many areas, on December 21, 1840 a letter to *The Cambrian* expressed the opinion that, while Welsh may be as good as English, the tide was running against it. The writer believed that prize money offered for literary compositions in Welsh as the various societies would be better used for translations and publications of "old works of genius and learning." The whole controversy, of course, was greatly stirred up by the appearance, in 1847, of the Report of The Blue Books. Over one hundred and fifty years later, the controversy was still continuing unabated.

A massive decline in the use of Welsh took place in the Valleys of South Wales during the first half of the twentieth century. Since the late 1960's, however, aided by the great increase in the number of Welsh primary schools, the number of children speaking the language has been increasing yearly. There may be cause for a quiet optimism for the future of the language in that most anglicized part of the country, despite mother Jane Thomas's request to her son to "Place to writ the next letter in Enlish." (sic)

(Note: on the author's visit to Ystradgylais in 1999, he found Welsh still very much in evidence as a living tongue).

Chapter Twelve:

David Thomas, Industrial Giant

When the *Roscius* finally docked in New York, David was still too ill to explore the city. His fever was still strong upon him. He had wanted to compare New York's grand buildings and parks with those he had seen briefly at Liverpool, but instead, as soon as he had disembarked with his family at Castle Gardens, at the foot of Manhattan, he found himself in the care of a doctor.

David's first month on American soil was spent in a hospital in New Brighton, Staten Island, attended by Dr Harcourt, the quarantine physician. Poor Elizabeth was dumbfounded by the strange tongues she heard in the hospital and in the city. She could not understand a single word spoken by the doctor and his nursing staff and was completely unable to follow the instructions for her husband's care. Where were all the Welsh settlers she had heard about? Thank heavens the children had been learning English at school in Ystradgynlais before they sailed.

At last David recovered sufficiently to undertake the land journey to Philadelphia, where he was to meet with the members of the Board of the Crane Company, set up especially to utilize his experience and talents. The family traveled by rail to New Brunswick, in New Jersey, and then by stage coach into Pennsylvania. Their business completed, after spending one night at Easton, where they met the representatives of the Lehigh Company, they reached Allentown on July 9.

In this little town of about 2,500 inhabitants, they managed to find a place on Front Street to reside for four months while a house was being built for them on Second and Pine Streets. It was situated close to the new works being constructed especially to receive his experiments with iron ore and anthracite. Only two days after their arrival, David and Samuel, his youngest son, who was then thirteen years old, went out to survey the land at Biery's Bridge, the site chosen for the new furnace and the factory and township that were to follow.

As soon as he was able, David wrote to George Crane to tell him of the state of his health and the situation in the New World as far as his plans were concerned. Crane's letter of reply came back very quickly. He stated that he was so glad that all was well with the family; that David's illness could only have been expected considering the nature of an Atlantic crossing.

David's early letters provided Crane with a great deal of information concerning the iron trade in America. In reply, Crane stated that he believed that shortly they would be witnessing a great start in the iron trade of the United States in which his former steward would be taking a distinguished part. He was gratified to find that Mr. Hazard and "the Lehigh people" had treated the newcomers as he felt certain they would.

Crane wrote that the bricks and castings that David needed to begin construction of his new furnace in Pennsylvania were all gone (i.e. had all been sent on to Thomas); but of all the troublesome transactions they ever had with so small an affair, "the biggest pester" was in getting freight and having the cylinders for the furnace shipped to Thomas.

Crane stated that he had been plagued to death with shipping the necessary articles from that David so desperately needed to begin. He had written upwards of fifty letters to the "rascally captains," but was now tired of trying, though he had to confess that he could see that they did not like to risk having such heavy castings upon deck; and none of them would consent to have their holds widened to receive them.

The two blast cylinders were still lying at Cardiff Docks in Wales as the captain of the vessel refused to allow them aboard as being too large for the hold. Only 4 inches needed to be cut to fit them, wrote Crane, and a Mr. Gerald Ralston had offered to pay for the "injury" to the ship; they had even begged that the captain might assist in getting the cylinders shipped by another vessel. As Thomas's new furnace would not be in blast before the spring, Crane was quite sure the cylinders should arrive some months before they were needed.

But Crane's hopes did not materialize. What eventually happened was that the ship bringing the necessary parts for the furnace was also loaded with iron rails from South Wales for the Lehigh Company; and just after it arrived in the United States and was cleared for Philadelphia, it sprang a leak and had to put in to Norfolk, Virginia in distress. About 300 tons of rails were jettisoned.

Mr. Erskine Hazard and David Thomas journeyed to Norfolk to receive the cylinders, only to find that they were still sitting on the dock in Wales. The ship's captain "more forceful than eloquent" then told them that if the castings had not been so heavy, they too would have gone overboard along with the rails. After repairs, the ship did reach Philadelphia and most of the material from Britain for the building of the first furnace at Catasauqua was shipped by canal to the Crane works

Many years later, in his Reminiscences, Samuel stated that it had not been Mr. Hazard who had undertaken the responsibility of procuring the necessary machinery and other appliances for the erection of the furnace in Pennsylvania.

The whole matter had been placed in the hands of David Thomas, and for the four months that he had remained in Wales following his agreement with the Lehigh Company, David had made all the arrangements for the entire outfit of the furnace. He had the blowing machinery constructed at the Soho Works, in England; and the hot blasts at Ynyscedwyn, in Wales, under the supervision of John Clee, who was to be David's successor as superintendent.

One great problem facing David upon his arrival in eastern Pennsylvania had been the lack of foundry facilities in the area, but finally, the large cast-iron center pieces, segments, gudgeons and pinions for the water wheel were made at the Allentown Foundry of Brobst and Barber, the same foundry at which the first steam engine in Lehigh County was erected (now lovingly preserved at the campus of Lafayette College, Easton, Pa).

Tapping the furnace at Catasauqua, Pa., late 19th century

Historian Peckitt tells how David planned to replace the cylinders that were still in Wales. He first applied to the Alger Works at Boston; to the Allaire Works, and the Morgan Iron Works of New York, but all declined to undertake the work; they were unable to bore cylinders of that size and were unwilling to enlarge their mills for the purpose. No mill in the United States at that time could bore a cylinder 60" in diameter.

Thomas then tried Merrick and Towne of the Southwark Foundry in Philadelphia, who enlarged their boring mill and complete the work, charging 12.5 cents a pound for the finished cylinders, which were fitted to the tops and bottoms sent from Britain and erected in place.

Too late to be used in the original furnace at Catasauqua, the original cylinders finally arrived from Cardiff in 1840 and were duly employed. One of them was washed down stream by the great flood of 1841 and lodged in a deep gully. Both were later used in the construction of two blowing engines erected at Number One Furnace and were in use for several years.

In 1868 the cylinders were taken to Alburtus near Allentown to be used in the new, large furnace erected there to supplement the small furnace at the Lock Ridge Iron Company (the capital stock of which had been bought by the rapidly expanding Thomas Iron Company). These original cylinders were still in use as late as 1899.

In a letter of October 17, 1839 George Crane wrote that he was glad Mr. Thomas had written in such fine spirits and should it please God to continue him in health, Crane has no doubts that the all the expectations formed by both of them will be realized. "In your own age," he writes, "you will see how necessary it is for persons to go out when very young to enable their constitution to fit themselves to the climate."

In actuality, the difficulties faced by Thomas in addition to his illness had been enormous. Apart from the difficulties with the English ship captains, he acknowledged freely that there had been other delays, discouragements and difficulties on every side. Thomas himself was ill for weeks in the Fall, which greatly impeded the progress of the work. Samuel, his youngest son, was used as a messenger to those in charge of construction during his father's illness. The work had continued.

In the October letter, Crane states that he had heard of William Lyman's problems in Pennsylvania, but that he fully expected that because of the "judicious advice" David had given him (Lyman) with respect to the stoves, better luck would attend his next attempt." Apparently, Thomas had unselfishly given Lyman detailed plans for the construction of a complete furnace, operated under Crane's patent.

Lyman was honored in 1840 for being the first person in the United States to make anthracite pig iron continuously for 100 days (he had blown in the first furnace at Pottsville, Pennsylvania, on January 18, 1840). It had been taken over by Benjamin Perry, yet another immigrant from Wales, producing about 28 tons a week of good foundry iron.

Though it managed to produce good-quality iron for about three months, the Pioneer was not a technical success, despite the award given to Lyman. It lacked the correct mixture of furnace size, blast temperature and pressure, and all the other elements that Thomas was able to combine successfully in his own experiments. The need for someone with David's experience and management skills still existed.

It is a great tribute to David's magnanimity that he so freely gave of his expertise to George Lyman in those early, critical days, despite his own disappointments at not getting the shipments so necessary for his own work and the delays also caused by his ill health.

The same letter from George Crane contains some specific instructions for Thomas which were probably superfluous, considering the expertise the latter possessed. He was told to put in a full-sized hearth, as small hearths could often be obstructed by stone coal though the blast could easily find its way through coke.

One of the problems in constructing furnaces that utilized anthracite had been the design. Earlier furnaces had been designed for bituminous coal. Thomas's solution at Ynyscedwyn and later at Catasauqua was to build the throats of the furnaces much wider in diameter in proportion to the boshes.

With a narrower throat, the coal had partially disintegrated, detached pieces falling to the hearth and the accumulation of carbonaceous matter was a serious disadvantage. The larger throated furnaces greatly increased the facility of smelting with anthracite, which could be converted into a dense coke

The size determined upon by Thomas was a proper one, wrote Crane, 45 feet high with a 30 feet square base, but he was to erect the stoves right away for which the castings were sent out. The boshes (the narrow, angled interior sides of the furnace near the hearth) have to be kept steep: "15 feet from the top of the hearth will do."

Crane's letter continues with the detail that the money market in Britain was in a dreadful state, more than he had ever known it before, and this had greatly affected payments due his business. He also disclosed that an American iron master, Mr. Elicot, of Baltimore, had been visiting the Ynyscedwyn Works and had agreed that the iron produced there for boiler plates was fully equal to that produced by charcoal.

Crane then stated that he repeats his joy that David had started a new Sunday School in the new township. The letter ends with Crane's hope for David that "your exertions will be blest to the population around you for both worlds, more especially for that which will be for a never-ending eternity in duration."

Despite the delays caused by the refusal of the shipping companies to ship the blowing cylinders, Thomas had wasted no time in setting about erecting the first furnace projected by the company at Biery Bridge, "a place later named Catasauqua" (place of the burnt, bare grounds). The masonry was laid by Isaac McHose or Rittersville, whose own son Samuel was subsequently the builder of nearly all the furnaces in the Lehigh Valley. The original furnace was so well built and produced such good quality iron that it was still in use as late as 1876.

The ground for the furnace was broken for its construction in August, 1839. "After many first difficulties and discouragements," it was blown in at five o'clock on July 3, 1840. With two more recent Welshmen immigrants in charge, Williams Phillips and Evan Jones, the first run of iron came a day later, a cast

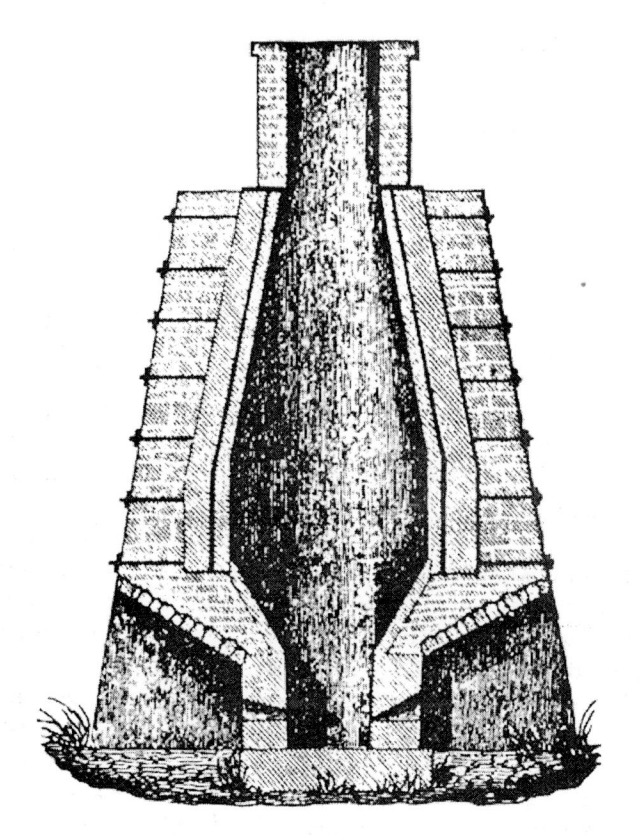

A 19th century blast furnace

of 4 tons. It was a pronounced success. What better day than the Fourth of July?

The Thomas furnace, "in which the success of the new discovery was first fully demonstrated in this country" was 42 ft in height, with 12 ft bosh. It was operated by a breast wheel 12 ft in diameter, driving two blowing cylinders worked by beams on a gallows frame, the power being supplied by the water of the canal — the difference between the upper and lower levels of lock No 36. The ore was two-thirds hematite to one-third New Jersey magnetic.

The first furnace remained in blast until the flood of January, 1841, that never did more than temporarily halt production, and during the first six months of its operation, it produced 1,080 tons of pig iron. When restarted after the flood, the furnace remained in blast from May 18, 1841 until August 6, 1842, producing 3,316 tons of pig iron. It was so well-designed and built that it was still producing good quality iron as late as 1876.

On August, 1840 one month after Thomas had blown in that important first furnace, he received a long letter from his former employer. In it, Crane states that he was happy to have received information from Thomas about the successful blowing in of the anthracite furnace at the Crane Iron Works in Pennsylvania and the application of the anthracite to the puddling and rolling processes.

Crane states that he has already shown to many persons who knew David "the success of his blowing- in the furnace." We can only imagine the excitement of both men at the implications of what they were doing in their respective countries. Crane was particularly excited that anthracite resembled charcoal in its analysis; he and David must have been wondering why it took so long for experienced iron masters to use it successfully in the manufacture of iron.

Crane added that he took great pleasure in acknowledging he has received intelligence concerning Thomas's success in puddling, etc with stone coal; he wrote, "I agree with you that one day you will see America a most important iron working country."

In another letter written the same month, Crane wonders what Mr. Hazard had to say about the iron now being produced at Catasauqua, and he wishes with all his heart that Thomas had been the first to start "the process" in America. Unfortunately, the problems with shipping the cylinders from Cardiff had upset everything.

Then follows a statement that is puzzling, for Crane gives no credit to David for the discovery they had surely worked out together. When America does become an important iron working country, he writes, "I hope that she will not forget that she must date at least her anthracite success to me, and so far as pecuniary returns, I hope that she will willingly (without giving me too much trouble) render 'tribute to whom tribute is due' — on that subject, I entertain but little apprehension on either side of the water." Because of Lyman's work, however, Crane was not honored in the United States in the way he thought he deserved.

The first Thomas furnace was quickly followed by many other iron masters in the state of Pennsylvania, some successful, some not. In the fall of 1840, following the success of Thomas, an American iron master named William Henry built an anthracite furnace on the Lackawanna, near present-day Scranton. He had great problems in procuring the necessary fire brick, blast machinery and hot blast apparatus from American manufacturers. Consequently, it was not until October of the following year that he could attempt the first blast, which turned out to be a total failure.

It was another Welsh immigrant ironworker, John F. Davies, who helped the Lackawanna Furnace finally become successful in 1842. By that time, the proven technical and management skills of David Thomas had kept him well in the forefront of developments in the iron industry, a position he was to keep for many years and which fully earned him the title of "Father of the American Anthracite Iron Industry."

In South Wales, there was great pride that David Thomas and his family had done so well in the United States, fulfilling all the hopes expressed by George Crane in those early letters to his former superintendent. Who among the workmen back at Ynyscedwyn or Neath Abbey would have thought that Dai the Stiward would have succeeded so admirably?

In February, 1842, Llewelyn Jeffreys wrote to his old friend from Defynog. He has received the joyful news that Thomas will be coming over to Wales in the summer. To that news he says "Amen, Amen," not only for himself, "but for the public at large whom had the pleasure of knowing you."

Mr Jeffreys then states that nothing has yet appeared that would prevent his going back with Thomas, for he was determined to go to America ere long, times being very bad indeed in Wales. He has no real cause to complain, however, for he has sixty pounds a year "exclusive the keeping of a cow and a horse, a horse and five free, as well as the two gardens which Thomas formerly had in his occupation — everything together being better than a hundred pounds."

Jeffreys considered this a very handsome salary, especially for such "a blunt" as himself. The previous week he had spoken to the Lord Lieutenant about David, about whom the latter had spoken very highly and whom he wished well wherever he resided.

While Llewelyn Jeffreys was relatively content with his lot, George Crane was not. He certainly was not having the same degree of success in Wales that David Thomas was enjoying in America, despite the proven quality of iron produced from anthracite at Ynyscedwyn and all the promise of the new industry and the part that Crane expected to play in it.

Lots of problems were ensuing from the fact that other companies were cashing in on what Crane considered to be his invention. Soon after his arrival in the United States, David received a letter from his former employer complaining of the considerable difficulties in having his patent enforced. Apparently the Neath Iron Works, where Thomas had once served his apprenticeship, had been using Crane's methods of smelting iron with anthracite by means of the hot blast, and the owner, Mr. Joseph Price, had not been paying Crane his royalty on the patent.

Accounts of the legal proceedings referred to as "Crane against the Neath Abbey Company" appear from time to time in *The Cambrian*. One of these described a meeting of the South Wales Anthracite Association at which was discussed "the most unfortunate and protracted suit between Crane and Mr. Price, of the Neath Company."

Crane had also filed a bill in Chancery against "the Ystalwern people" for the profits from their output of iron using his methods; his case with the Neath Abbey people, concerning their use of his patent, was still awaiting its turn. Though the case eventually came to trial in Westminster Hall in London in February, 1840 before the Lord Chief Justice and a special jury, judgment was not delivered until June 13, 1842.

These were not the only proceedings taking place. On September 17, 1841, John Walter's letter to David had included the information that Crane had lost his case against the Swansea Copper Company, and that "there was great joy at Swansea on account of it."

Sadly, Crane did not live much longer after the unfavorable decision; one evening, taking liniment in mistake for cough medicine, he accidentally poisoned himself. It was thus that he did not survive long enough to witness the showing of an Ynyscedwyn ingot of pig iron displayed at the Great

David Thomas' home at 2nd and Pine Sts, Catasauqua, Pennsylvania

Exhibition of 1851 at Crystal Palace, London.

In the latter part of 1842, the Lehigh Crane Company, under the direction of Thomas, decided to build its Number Two furnace that measured 34 feet at the base. It was 13 feet 4 inches at the bosh, and 45 feet high. Another canal had to be built as a feeder.

After the success of these furnaces at Catasauqua, anthracite furnaces began to multiply rapidly throughout eastern Pennsylvania. They were erected at Stanhope, Glendon, Harrisburg and Reading, so that by 1846 there were about forty such furnaces in operation on the Rivers Lehigh, Hudson, Susquehanna and Schuylkill.

In 1843, at the Number Two Furnace, David tried an experiment that Samuel believed was the first of its kind in the United States. This had the aim of utilizing the waste gases for refining iron, taking out the gas at a depth of some 9 feet below the top of the furnace instead of being taken out immediately under the dumping ring at the tunnel head. The practical purpose of the experiment was the refining and puddling of iron for making an extra quantity of bar iron and wire. It was precisely this kind of experiment that George Crane, back at Ynyscedwin, wanted Thomas to provide details of in his letters home.

The same year saw the construction of Furnace Number Three at Catasauqua, during which an argument developed as to what source of power should be used for blowing. Thomas argued for steam, stating that not enough water remained in the Lehigh River during the dry season to blow an additional furnace. Mr. White, who argued at first for water power, was defeated in the argument by Thomas, along with Hazard and Douglas, and steam was chosen for the new furnace.

This furnace was even larger than the others; it was 40 feet wide at the base, 17 feet bosh, and 47 feet high. In it, in 1847 an experiment was tried in which a strong electric current was passed through the molten iron to dispel the phosphorus, but after a nearly fatal accident, it was disbanded as no discernable difference was found in the quantity of iron.

At Catasauqua, Thomas built four more furnaces for the Lehigh Crane Company, all with a larger productive capacity than the first one. Other furnaces were added gradually, so that by 1870, the company's six stacks were producing about 100,000 tons of pig iron yearly, and the USA was far outstripping Wales in the manufacture of this important product. It is significant that over half the iron made in whole country came from Pennsylvania, principally in the valleys of the Lehigh, Schuylkill and Susquehanna Rivers.

Chapter Thirteen:
Papa Thomas Man of Mark.

The Anthracite Era which David Thomas set in motion almost as soon as he arrived in the United States was to last nearly 80 years before being displaced by the coming of steel manufacture at Pittsburgh and other centers. The Lockridge Funace at Albertus, Allentown, Pennsylvania, a site of one of the former Thomas works, records his and his dynastic family's achievements in the iron industry. It is indeed a story of a man of iron.

Still strong and active at 80 years old, David Thomas was elected President of the Inronmaster's Convention in Philadelphia. He died just before his 88th birthday on June 20, 1882. His family, which had been vaccinated, had survived the small pox epidemic that struck particularly hard at the Pennsylvania industrial communities.

At his funeral, testimony was given to David Thomas, "immigrant from Wales," as an honored and beloved national benefactor to the United States.

Inside the Thomas musuem, Lockridge, near Allentown, Pa.

His funeral procession, with 64 carriages, carrying "the elite of the Lehigh Valley" was a testimony to his influence and popularity in the district. Marching in front of the catafalque were 900 workmen from the iron furnaces of the Thomas Companies. David was buried in what was to become the family vault at Fairview Cemetary.

When Thomas first arrived at Allentown, he had been regarded as something of a visionary. One leading charcoal master told him, "I will eat all the iron you make with anthracite." And this seemed to express the general feeling of the trade at the time. The iron master did not keep his promise, however, even though Thomas later invited him to a hearty dinner cooked in the company's first, and successful, furnace.

Only ten years after his setting up shop at Catasauqua, Thomas received high praise as the one person who had been responsible for bringing prosperity to the Lehigh Valley. Ten years of feverish industry had resulted in the erection of an immense number of furnaces in the valley, supplied by stone coal alone. One writer described their proliferation in particularly glowing terms: "The perfection to which there have been brought is a security that nothing can check their prosperity, or prevent their extension in this country."

The author at the Thomas factory, Lockridge, Pennsylvania

The Thomas Ironworks at Lockridge, Pennsylvania, 1996

Thanks to Thomas, the Lehigh Valley, was transformed from a rural plantation-based system into a modern large scale enterprise. Many writers believe that its importance in the industrial history of America can be compared to that of the Severn Valley in Britain a century before. Both valleys became the world's center of iron production in their respective times.

In a letter to his niece Jane, written in March 1867, David Thomas mentions that Catasauqua had now over four thousand people, "and there was not one house here when I came 28 years ago, and there is a great many buildings gone up since last summer." Responsible for laying the first water mains in the community, he and his sons were building a new house 12 miles on the Railroad "from here to the Lehigh Mountain". The rolling mill was going full time, he wrote, and had much changed lately.

Of those early, heady times, in his *Reminiscences*, youngest son Samuel tells of a practical joke that he played on the whole town. At the time, the steam whistle was an unknown sound in the Lehigh Valley. Samuel had one made secretly by Mr. Lehman, a brass founder at Bethlehem. When Number Three furnace was ready, and the large whistle attached to the boilers, Samuel "let her off." The tremendous noise startled the whole town and occasioned much laughter. According to Samuel, some women gathered up their children in panic, thinking they had heard "The Last Trump."

At the time, when no facilities of telegraph, telephone existed, and US railroads were still in their infancy, not yet having reached the Lehigh or Wyoming Valleys in Pennsylvania, it took three whole days to transact business between the Crane Works and Philadelphia. Even as late at 1855, the only means of transporting coal from Mauch Chunk and magnetic ore from New Jersey was by canal. The hematite ores and limestone came by wagon, "the country literally swarming with teams." In that year, the Lehigh Valley Railroad opened, with David Thomas as one of the directors.

Until the Tariff Act of 1842, rails had been admitted into the United States virtually free of duty, but after the Act, the manufacture of the heavy iron rails for the great number of new railroads being constructed in so many areas of the United States began in earnest. In the decade of the 1830's progress was rapid; by 1840, there were almost 3,000 miles of track.

By 1854, over 17000 miles of railroad had been constructed in United States, and another 12000 miles were being built. On the eve of the Civil War, the number of miles had grown to 30,000. This totaled more railroad miles than existed in the rest of the world put together. Their impact has never been fully estimated, but the growth and prosperity they brought with them took industries and communities was simply enormous, far greater than had ever been anticipated by the early pioneers.

In 1844 at the Mt Savage Rolling Mill in Alleghany County the very first rail struck in the United States was one of the kind known in Wales as the Evans Rail, patent of the Dowlais Iron Works. The Montour Mills at Danville (where famous Welsh composer Joseph Parry was later to work as a young immigrant) were built in 1845 with the express purpose of rolling iron rails, and the demand soon lead to mills sprouting up everywhere to keep up the supply.

In 1854, when he was 60 years old, David Thomas formed the Thomas Iron Company at Hokendauqua on the Lehigh River. The streets were laid out on November 9, and the town named after the little creek that flows into the Lehigh. David's youngest son, Samuel was appointed as superintendent, following the young man's experience as the Crane Iron Works and in erecting an anthracite furnace at Boonton, New Jersey.

In 1855, David relinquished control of the Crane Works to devote his full time to his own works. Here, the production of pig iron per furnace was greater than that at any other iron works in the United States and perhaps in the entire world. The furnaces were the highest and the largest and had the most powerful blast machinery in the country. In its performance, the company was not only the largest in Pennsylvania, but also known as a model of good management and practice.

During the years 1855 to 1875, more iron was produced in the US with anthracite than by any other fuel. The Civil War certainly aided the expansion of the industry. In a letter dated 29 June, 1864, David's son writes of the price of iron being very high. They were selling their pig iron at 8 pounds ten a ton, or 45 dollars, and two new furnaces were being built at Hokendauqua.

Later in the same year in a letter he sent to Wales, David mentions his family's return from a 4-week tour of Canada and New England, including a trip up Mt Washington, in New Hampshire. Because of the war, "in which Sherman had just taken Atlanta," he states, iron prices were very high; pig iron was now 70 dollars a ton and bar iron "from our new rolling mills" was selling for 200-220 dollars a ton. Laboring men were earning two to two and a half dollars a day "and everything is still rising." David expresses his desire to return to visit his friends at Neath when possible, but not this summer as "times are very exciting and the exchange (rate) so very high."

That was not the only summer that David was too busy to return home. During his long, illustrious career, he became a director of many ironworks, coal mines and railroads. He returned to Wales only once during his lifetime. In 1866, he unsuccessfully contested as a Republican candidate for Congress, (declining on principle to take part in the canvass) presided over the Ironmaster's Convention in Philadelphia in 1874, and with his wife, celebrated his 65th wedding anniversary.

In a letter written in 1868, David mentions his retirement from the industry in which he had played such a prominent part. He wrote that he was simply attending to his own private affairs, as he "has finished his day's work and is awaiting the Master's call." He adds that the company now has five furnaces at Hokendauqua and are building two more.

David continued that he felt he was now too old to cross the ocean to visit

Neath. He promised to hire the young man from Briton Ferry (near Swansea) who had been introduced through his niece Jane's letter "as soon as the rolling mill starts up, but at present, men are all on strike through this part of the country." The mill owners were all reducing wages and the men contest it, but will no doubt have to give way as iron is getting very low here and labour will have to come down."

David added that he had sent some money for Jane to buy a footstool and a cushion for use in chapel and stated that he would send more back to Wales, but "it is a little far to give money to churches so far away." "Calls at home," he continues, "are loud and often, we have spent on our church this year two thousand pounds, over ten thousand dollars to beautify it and enlarge it." Two years ago, he had given them an organ that cost over six hundred pounds, and "you will admit I know that charity begins at home."

The Thomas Iron Works, Hokendauqua, Pennsylvania, earlt 1900's

In 1869, David was seventy-five years old. In a letter to *The Literary Album*, he stated that all his early experiments in the use of anthracite to smelt iron ore had resulted in a loss (in Wales) of pounds, shillings, and pence as well as in dollars and cents in the U.S. He went on to say "without fear of contradiction, that I made the first anthracite iron that yielded a recompense unto those who invested their capital in the manufacture of it; and I have lived long enough to see about tw-pthrids or three-fourths of all the iron made in this country made with anthracite coal as fuel."

In one early letter from George Crane, the writer had concluded by asking David to tell his three that if they proved to be good boys, they would become men of importance in America. It did happen that all David's sons were trained to take on responsibilities and management duties at the company and at other iron works. In the words of one American newspaper, they were all truly "chips off the old block."

Unfortunately, David was killed at the age of 25 while erecting a boiler stack for furnace Nr 4 at Hockendauqua, but both John and Samuel became important, innovative and influential leaders in the American iron industry. Their paternal interest in the welfare of their work force was proverbial, and they were heavily involved in the religious, educational, and social aspects of the communities connected with the iron works. Samuel became the 2nd vice-president of the Hokendauqua Works, followed by his brother John, who later left his position as manager of the Lehigh-Crane Company to fulfill an ambition to build an iron works in Alabama at a place later called Thomas in his honor.

By the year 1892, the Pennsylvania anthracite coal fields were producing 40 million tons a year. During David's supervision, the Thomas enterprise was easily the leading anthracite iron producer in the United States, and for many years its prices set the market for pig iron. In its heyday, the Thomas Iron Company had 13 blast furnaces in operation, backed by ownership of collieries, iron ore mines, and limestone quarries. It also possessed on of the largest rolling mills in the state and a large fire brick company.

In 1904, at the fiftieth anniversary of the Thomas Iron Works, there were nine active stacks in operation. The company had earned a reputation for high class foundry work as well as for basic and mill iron and could point with pride to a record of fifty years during which they had used an all-ore mixture.

The Thomas Iron Works also claimed to be the oldest company in America manufacturing pig iron that had not been reorganized or had its original corporate name changed since its beginning. In the early 1920's the company was still producing 260, 000 tons of iron a year from five active furnaces. It finally ceased operation in 1922.

From all we know of David Thomas, he was an extremely modest person. It was left to his son Samuel to take upon himself the duty of establishing the claims of his father to the successful application of anthracite to the production of pig iron in the United States. Samuel believed that his father did not assert himself more emphatically due to his modest and lack of means and influence to obtain a patent — no small undertaking at the time.

"With all due respects to George Crane, "stated Samuel, "he was in no sense of the world a mechanic or a technical man, but a shrewd business man, with a faculty for recognizing the merits and promoting the commercial application of the inventions of others — a faculty which is essential to the industrial progress as the genius of the investigator and inventor."

In his summary of the accomplishments of his father, Samuel stated: "It has never been claimed that no anthracite pig iron had been made in this country previous to 1840, but only that the commercial success of this manufacture dated from my father's work at Ynyscedwyn in 1837 and at Catasauqua in 1840. I have the highest authority for the statement that no so much as 500 tons of anthracite pig iron was made in this country during the entire experimental period preceding 1840."

Thomas's furnaces were the first of all those in the United States that were completely successful from both and engineering and a commercial standpoint, and Thomas subsequently became identified with the manufacture of anthracite pig iron than any of his contemporaries. There is every reason to agree with those nineteenth century writers who called David Thomas the "Father of the American anthracite iron industry," and to concur with those writing much more recently, who argue that David Thomas should be recognized as one of the most influential men in the growth of American industry in the 19th century.

The Author

REVIEWS OF RECENT BOOKS FROM GLYNDŴR PUBLISHING

100 GREAT WELSHMEN - T.D. Breverton ISBN 1-903529-034 £18.99, 376 pages, illustrated, edition limited to 900 copies (Glyndŵr Publishing)
Welsh Books Council 'Book of the Month' June 2001

Review from The Western Mail, May 11th 2001:
'New Book springs some surprises on history's greatest Welshmen:
POETS, PRESIDENTS AND A PIRATE TO BOOT
The lives of some of Wales' most famous figures are set out in a new book published today. Terry Breverton's new book *100 Great Welshmen* celebrates the achievements of 100 men of Welsh blood who have left their mark on history.
It contains the names of four American presidents, Hollywood superstars, Christian saints and some of the political and cultural minds who have shaped the modern world. Some, like Dylan Thomas and Owain Glyndŵr, immediately spring to mind, but others to make the list include great architects Frank Lloyd Wright and John Nash, and Confederate president Jefferson Davis. Below are just some of the famous names to make the list. The list is in alphabetical order......

Part of a double-page Review from the Western Mail Magazine, June 1st 2001
'...100 Great Welshmen is a revealing volume illustrating the great and the good with Welsh connection, either by birth or family ancestry. Admittedly all the usual suspects are included - Richard Burton, Tom Jones, Sir Geraint Evans, Gareth Edwards, Gwynfor Evans, Idris Davies, Aneurin Bevan, Jimmy Wilde and Saunders Lewis. But probably the most fascinating are the ones we either tend to forget are Welsh, or had no prior knowledge of their Celtic connection in the first place. John Adams, the first occupant of the White House; father of the American Revolution Samuel Adams; revolutionary Oliver Cromwell; cinematic pioneer D.W. Griffith; comedian Tommy Cooper, the list goes on and on. From heroes of Waterloo and computer engineers to lethal pirates and gold champions, Breverton has attempted to include them all, and that's no mean feat given our colourful heritage. Hats off to him for the painstaking research involved in every single one, a trademark which is typical of his previous work in "An A-Z of Wales and the Welsh", followed by "The Book of Welsh Saints" and "The Secret Vale of Glamorgan", all printed in Wales....'

Review from Ninnau (US) by Dr Peter Willams
'Now and again a book comes along that answers most, if not all your questions about your Welsh heritage. Who are the Welsh, who are their military heroes, political leaders, writers, poets, kings, princes, saints, historians, explorers, men of industry, famous actors, athletes, and religious leaders? T.D. Breverton, who gave us The Book of Welsh Saints and An A-Z of Wales and the Welsh, has provided the answers in his latest body of knowledge: a single volume with the informative title l00 Great Welshmen. The author includes not only those who have contributed so much to the making of Wales, but also many personalities who made their mark on American history. The single volume reference book gives biographical information on those persons of Welsh descent whom became influential in the political and industrial life of the United States, such as Presidents John Adams, John Quincy Adams, James Monroe, and Thomas Jefferson; the father of the American Revolution Samuel Adams; business tycoon J.P. Morgan, film pioneer D.W.Griffith, explorers John Evans and Meriwether Lewis and so on. The author even includes those terrors of the high seas, Black Bart, the infamous

pirate, and Captain Henry Morgan. The amount of research that went into the making of this book is astounding; it seems that the author left no stone unturned in order to ferret out information concerning his subjects. He has produced a veritable gold mine of a book that you can dip into again and again. 100 Great Welshmen will make you proud of your Welsh heritage by reminding you that the little country of Wales has contributed so much to the modern world in so many different areas...'

100 GREAT WELSH WOMEN - T.D. Breverton ISBN 1 903529 042 £16.99 304pp illustrated, edition limited to 900 copies

Review from The Daily Mirror, November 19, 2001 by Jason Lamport

'....Kylie reckons she inherited her singing ability from Maestag-born mum Carol Jones, who emigrated to Australia aged just 10. Kylie has travelled to Wales to visit her gran - who she affectionately calls 'nain' - Welsh for grandmother. Terry's book lists the top women of all time including queens, politicians and stars of stage and screen. Charlotte Church is there for 'flying the Welsh flag' on trips to meet American presidents and the Pope. Butetown superstar Shirley Bassey and Cardiff paralympic gold medallist Tanni Grey-Thomspon also make the book...'

Review from South Wales Echo, November 17, 2001 by Mark Stead
Welsh Girl Power Through The Ages

It's not often you see Charlotte Church and Catrin Glyndŵr - daughter of one of Wales' favourite sons, Owain - in the same list. Or Shirley Bassey and Tanni Grey-Thompson rubbing shoulders with Elizabeth Tudor, who ranks among England's greatest monarchs, and Gwenllian. But that's exactly where you'll find them in a new book celebrating Wales' most fascinating females. Author and publisher Terry Breverton, who estimates he has written over a million words in two years - launces his latest work, 100 Great Welsh Women, next week. The result of another extensive trawl through time, it celebrates the achievements of Welsh women through the ages.
Terry, from St Athan, lectures at UWIC, but most of his recent spare time has been spent penning a string of books - An A-Z of Wales and the Welsh, The Secret Vale of Glamorgan, The Book of Welsh Saints and 100 Great Welshmen have all hit bookshelves in the last two years. And he hopes his labours of love will help bring the pride back into Welsh history. 'All my books have been about the culture and heritage of Wales, because it is not taught in schools and politicians are not interested in it', he says. 'If we don't know our history, how are we supposed to attract tourists? When I came back here to live five years ago, I couldn't find anything to show my children what being Welsh means, so I decided if nobody else was going to do it, I would do it myself. I find the Welsh attitude to history very disappointing. Nobody seems interested in it, and I believe that's because we have been put down for so long, we believe and have accepted we are second-class citizens. We've even allowed our greatest hero - King Arthur - to be hijacked by the West Country.
Terry believes the tales of Welsh heroes and heroines needs to be told to a wider audience, and hopes his books will recover some lost ground. 'We've had Braveheart - why can't the same thing be done about the lives of Owain Glyndŵr and Owain Llawgoch?' he asks. The achievements of the women profiled in Terry's latest book stretch from the first century to the present day. 'Some of the women in the book were born outside Wales but considered themselves Welsh,' Terry explains. 'My criteria were that all of them must have done something for Wales and felt something for Wales. 'When I was researching 100 Great Welshmen, I kept coming across the achievements

of these Welsh women, so that's how the book started.'
The journey through time starts with Wales' greatest saints, many of whom were women, and continues through the stories of Elizabeth Tudor, Gwenllian, Boadicea, Petula Clark, Laura Ashley, Shirley Bassey, Mary Quant, Sian Phillips, George Eliot, Elizabeth David, Delia Smith and modern-day icons such as Tanni Grey-Thompson and Catherine Zeta-Jones. 'Tanni is such an interesting character, but she kept telling me she wasn't good enough to be included,' laughs Terry. The book also lifts the lid on some hidden stories - such as the Welsh woman who was the mother of the first Bishop of Rome, and the Pembrokeshire lady who was the unacknowledged Queen of England.
'I've tried to do them all justice and, to some extent, to set the record straight,' says Terry. 'Wales has a great tradition of female equality dating back well before the laws drawn up in the 10th century. Females have never been considered inferior to males, and Welsh people have always looked up to their mothers as much as their fathers.'
Hard work or not, Terry has no intention of resting on his laurels as far as books are concerned. 'Next up are a Welsh Almanac and a book on Welsh pirates,' he says. 'After all, the world's most successful pirate, Black Bart Roberts, was from Pembrokeshire, the world's most cunning pirate, Hywel Davies, was Welsh, and so was the world's most famous buccaneers, Captain henry Morgan, after whom the rum is named. I have always wanted to find out more about these people, and there should be societies devoted to them, but instead it seems we ignore everything about the past... the book is launched at Oriel Bookshop, Cardiff, with a poetry reading from Ruth Bidgood and music from singer-songwriter and actress Amy Wadge....*

South Wales Echo, November 17, 2001
A Vale of Glamorgan author is making headline with a new book in which Kylie Minogue rubs shoulders with the Virgin Queen, Elizabeth I, and Catherine Zeta Jones. 100 Great Welsh Women, Terry Breverton's companion piece to 100 Great Welsh Men, details the cream of Welsh womenhood from the past 2000 years and includes saints, queens, athletes and actresses. Alongside familiar national figures such as Charlotte Church and Shirley Bassey, some choices such as Kylie, Hollywod actress Bette Davies and top cook Delia Smith have been causing a stir in the Welsh media. Mr Breverton, 55, a senior business lecturer at UWIC, said: The women did not have to have been born in Wales but to have benefited Wales to be categorised as 'great'. The author of such previous titles as The Secret Vale of Glamorgan and The Book of Welsh Saints is no stranger to controversy after claiming that Elvis Presley had Welsh ancestry in his book An A-Z of Wales and the Welsh.

THE BOOK OF WELSH SAINTS - T.D. Breverton ISBN 1-903529-018 £24.99 hardback, 606 pages, illustrated, edition limited to 900 copies (Glyndur Publishing)

Review from 'Cambria', January 2001:
'Another work from the prolific pen of Terry Breverton who is blazing a trail in producing bodies of knowledge about Welsh heritage and history. The Book of Welsh Saints is **an enormous work of research and will provide a welcome and ready book of reference** to the men and women who in Tad Deiniol's words "created Wales". The much bandied term "The Dark Ages" may well have meant just that east of the Severn, but to us this period is the Age of Saints. And there are hundreds of them - over 900 in fact - monks, scholars, warriors, missionaries. Breverton places Arthur firmly in the context of Welsh history and shows how the seminal folk legends of European romance

and literature originate in Wales. We see Wales at the very heart and very root of western Christian civilisation, a pre-eminent position...

e-mail from Dr Rowan Williams, Archbishop of Wales:
...*the book is a really extraordinary achievement: a compilation of tradition, topography and literary detective work that can have few rivals. I have enjoyed browsing in enormously, and have picked up all sorts of new lines to follow up...*'

Meic Stephens, in 'The Western Mail Magazine', April 7th, 2001
An even more impressive work is Terry Breverton's Book of Welsh Saints, which lists over 900 saints - those holy men who lived as ascetics and hermits in the first centuries after Christ and to whom, so often, miracles were attributed. These men were the first representatives of Rome in Celtic Britain and their names and places of worship still reverberate throughout our history and dot the landscape, reminding ourselves of a civilisation which went into the making of the Welsh landscape. There are informative notes on Saint Cewydd (the Welsh equivalent of St Swithin), Patrick (who became the patron saint of Ireland), and many another saint remembered only because there is a village called Llan, followed by his name. (I am reminded that the awful, corrupted name Llantwit seems to be named after a saint called Twit - surely its time the people of that splendid village rose up and demanded the correct form Illtud). The book was written with one eye on the potential tourist market, because it argues in favour of celebrating the saints' days in villages the length of Wales...'

Review from Ninnau (US) by Dr Peter Williams
'*Did you know that Wales had a St Elvis?...According to local tradition, St David was baptised by his cousin St Elvis at a church near Solva, in Pembrokeshire, where St Elvis Parish is now the smallest in Britain. Within the parish is also St Elvis farm, St Elvis Holy Well, St Elvis Cromlech (prehistoric tomb). Off the coast at Solva are St Elvis Rocks. St Elvis is only one of the hundred of Welsh saints of the 5th and 6th century, a time when the light of Christianity shone brightly in Wales when it had been extinguished over all of Europe, a time when England was still pagan. It was a time when Christianity itself was in danger of disappearing, the survival of the Church in Wales creating a bastion from which Ireland was first converted, and from the Irish missionaries, the rest of Britain and Europe.
Over 100 Welsh saints are associated with the leader Arthur, long before the legends had taken hold in France. It was a time when the stories of Arthur and Guinevere, of the Holy Grail, Tristan and Isolde, The Fisher King, the Black Knight, the Green Knight and all of the great and famous knights associated with Camelot and Avalon came into being, and all originated in Wales. Wales certainly seems to have not only the oldest surviving language in Europe, but also the oldest Christian heritage; for the first millennium, it was accepted by Rome as "the cradle of the Western Church".
The unique historical importance of Wales has for too long been neglected until now...the book lists over 900 saints, gives not only their history but the historical background of each saint, their feast-days and feast Weeks, and the religious events associated with them. The book is a veritable goldmine of information. Its appendices give the derivation of Welsh place-names, the location of Roman sites in Wales, a discussion of the language problem, and even an essay on the state of parliamentary representation in Wales. The book is a must for anyone interested in the history of the Church in Wales, indeed for anyone interested in learning the glorious heritage bequeathed to them from the time when Wales was the only Christian country in the world.*'

THE DRAGON ENTERTAINS - 100 Welsh Stars - Alan Roderick ISBN 1-903529-026 £12.99 paperback, illustrated 230 pages, edition limited to 900 copies (Glyndur Publishing)

The Dragon Entertains is a reference book with a difference - a highly readable, informative account of the lives of One Hundred Welsh Stars. Within its pages the reader will find 100 concise mini-biographies, word pictures detailing all the relevant, basic facts of the entertainer's career. For a small country, on the western fringe of Europe, a nation of only 3,000,000 people, Wales' contribution to the world of entertainment is immense. Actors and actresses, playwrights and directors, singers and musicians, composers and comedians - Wales has produced them all. And what other nation of comparable size can boast four Oscar winners? The first Welsh film star, the Welsh influence on the *James Bond* movies, *Monty Python*, *Dr Who*, *The Goon Show*, the Beatles films and the original Angry Young man can all be found in the pages of Alan Roderick's new book. Stars of Broadway and the West End stage, the Silver Screen, television, radio, the worlds of opera and contemporary rock music - *The Dragon Entertains* has them all. Welsh-speaking and non-Welsh-speaking, North Wales and South Wales - Welsh showbiz life in all its many facets can be found here.

Review by Meic Stephens, The Western Mail Magazine, January 2001
Lastly, another book published by Wales books, The Dragon Entertains (£12.99) by Alan Roderick, a highly-readable reference work listing 100 of the most famous Welsh stars of stage, screen and radio, from The Alarm to the TV comedian, Ronnie Williams. The list is a roll-call of the theatrical talent that Wales has produced over the last century: Ivor Novello, Tommy Cooper, Donald Houston, Donald Peers, Emlyn Williams from among the dead. And Tom Jones, Anthony Hopkins, Bryn Terfel, the Super Furry Animals, Harry Secombe, Kenneth Griffiths, Victor Spinetti and Max Boyce among the gloriously alive and still performing. It also includes fascinating information about the Welsh connections of stars like Glen Ford, Bob Hope, Rolf Harris, Griff Rhys Jones and Petula Clark.
This is the book to reach for the next time someone tells you that Wales has not nurtured any great talent in the world of entertainment and showbiz.

THE SECRET VALE OF GLAMORGAN - T.D. Breverton ISBN 1-903529-00X £13.99 paperback, illustrated 230 pages, edition limited to 400 copies (Glyndur Publishing)

In between what may be the oldest university in Europe, and a cradle of early Christianity, Llanilltud Fawr (Llantwit Major), and another shining monastic light from the Dark Ages, the Welsh *Age of Saints*, lies the village of Sain Tathan. From the introduction of this millennium history, we read:
'We tend to think of where we live as unremarkable, compared to the strangeness of the new. However, the village of St Tathan and the hamlets of Flemingston, Gileston, Eglwys Brewys and West and East Aberthaw are not only attractive, and set in wonderful countryside, but have a history almost unique in such a small area. We have buzzards, kingfishers and partridge, the Heritage Coast, two deserted villages, four mediaeval churches, three conservation areas, traces of rebellion by the great Welsh heroes Llywelyn Bren and Owain Glyndur, Roman remains, the great antiquary Iolo Morganwg who reintroduced the Eisteddfod to Wales, mediaeval wells, four sixth

century saints, an astronomer consulted by Sir Isaac Newton, a Rebecca Rioter, the remains of a thriving port, wreckers, ghosts, smugglers, West Indies slave-ships, hymn-writers, a thatched 14th century pub and no less than four castles. In the 1980's even a Humpback Whale visited...

Review by Meic Stephens, in 'The Western Mail Magazine', April 7th, 2001
Terry Breverton belongs t that rare breed of Welshmen who stake their livelihood on trying to publish books in which they passionately believe. His imprint Glyndŵr Publishing/Wales Books has already made its mark on the Welsh publishing scene by bringing out substantial and handsomely produced books on Welsh subjects, particularly local history. He was born in the Vale of Glamorgan, to which he has returned after many years as a management consultant in Britain and overseas. He is the author of several useful books such as An A-Z of Wales and the Welsh and One Hundred Great Welshmen. What drives him as a publisher is the belief that the Welsh people have been deprived of their own history. He aims to provide the information that will make them proud of their country. If that means he has to lose some money, he thinks it's well worth it. Among his most recent books is The Secret Vale of Glamorgan (Glyndŵr, £13.99) which shows a local man's pride in the history and culture of his native patch, combined with a historian's delight in tracing the past and relating it to the present. For anyone born or living in the Vale, this book should be essential reading. There are chapters on Cowbridge, St Athan, Gileston, Aberthaw, Flemingston, and all the places in between, together with a wealth of information about the area's most famous son, the wayward genius Iolo Morganwg.

A RHONDDA BOY - Ivor Howells - ISBN 1-903529 050 £6.99 paperback 144 pages, 33 illustrations. A charming evocation of his childhood in Porth, Rhondda, and summer holidays in Ferryside, by the 93 year-old former headmaster of Porth and Tonypandy Secondary Schools, edited and researched by his former colleague Owen Vernon Jones.

FORTHCOMING TITLES

Spring 2002 - The Path to Inexperience
June 2002 - Glyn Dwr's War - The Campaigns of the Last Prince of Wales
June 2002 - The Welsh Almanac
September 2002 - The Book of Welsh Pirates and Buccaneers
Autumn 2002 - Owain Llawgoch - the History of a Legend
Autumn 2002 - The Quilt of Dreams
Autumn 2002 - The Journals of Llewellin Penrose - Seaman
Winter 2002 - Another 100 Great Welshmen
Winter 2002 - Wales and the Welsh - the New A-Z
Spring 2003 - Madoc - the Evidence
Spring 2003 - The Glamorgan Heritage Coast
Summer 2003 - The Castles of Wales Volume I - Glamorgan
Summer 2003 - Welsh Entrepreneurs
Winter 2003 - Arthur ap Meurig ap Tewdrig
Summer 2004 - Yet Another 100 Great Welshmen
Winter 2004 - True Brits - the History of the British Peoples

WALES BOOKS AND GLYNDWR PUBLISHING ARE NON-PROFIT-MAKING ENTERPRISES DEDICATED TO PUBLISHING BOOKS UPON WALES, ITS HERITAGE, CULTURE AND HISTORY. Our (non-subsidised) books are all produced in Wales, and are available via the Welsh Books Council, direct from the publisher, from walesbooks.com or from 'good' book shops. Our publications all have a two-fold purpose - to tell the world about Wales and encourage tourism, and to tell the Welsh people what they have never been taught in schools, colleges and universities. The Welsh legacy has been deliberately suppressed for hundreds of years, and publication policy is to open up the truth about their past to the Welsh people. Without culture, a nation cannot exist. Without a knowledge of its culture, a nation will quickly die - there is nothing to hold it together.

TORFAEN LIBRARIES